TURN STRATEGY INTO ACTION

Strategic Project Management Tools for Leaders and Teams

---

*Reach Goals Faster and Smoother
with the Logical Framework Approach*

Terry Schmidt

Copyright © 2007 Terry Schmidt
Turn Strategy Into Action:
Strategic Project Management Tools for Leaders and Teams
Strategic Mastery Press
1st Edition

Library of Congress Control Number: 2007934909
ISBN: 0-9772808-2-9

Substantial discounts on bulk quantities of these books are available to corporations, government agencies, professional associations, and other organizations.

For details and discount information, contact: info@ManagementPro.com.

Praise for Turn Strategy Into Action

"We used this method to organize and execute an Awards campaign that earned numerous nominations and awards, including an Oscar®."

– Don Levy, Senior Vice President, Sony Pictures Digital

"Terry has created a powerful and actionable methodology for change. Our team at eBay got immersed in it, loved it, and have taken it to heart. I'm definitely adding this valuable tool to my management toolbelt!"

– Arnold Goldberg, Senior Director, Systems Engineering, eBay

"Terry's books guide your thinking about any reasonably complex goal you're trying to achieve. I've seen very few things in this space that make sense past the paper they're written on. This is a remarkable exception."

– David Allen, Author,
Getting Things Done: The Art of Stress-Free Productivity

"Your system is simple and practical for use in work and in life. I use this with my work team to improve productivity, and to plan my career and family future."

– Wanchai Sri-Isaraporn, General Manager, Toyota Motor Thailand Co., Ltd

"Pound for pound, Terry is the world's best strategic project consultant."

– Joseph Sumo, Project Manager, Boeing

"Anyone charged with project responsibility will benefit from reading this book. These easy to follow steps to turn strategy into action will really make a positive difference."

Jeffrey M. Chase, PhD, Chairman, National Traffic Safety Institute

"Terry provides a clear and compelling methodology for creating enterprise-wide strategies that integrate all of our sub-departments. This is a must read book for any leader who wants to revitalize their organization."

– Dale Hough, Chief of Reengineering, Los Angeles County Assessor Office

"As an engineer, I'm reluctant to get all weepy about management processes, but your model is a logical and demonstrably effective tool for organizing and executing complex strategies."

– David Sanders, Engineer, TRW

"Learn from a master as Terry offers practical hands-on tools for tackling the tough issues that keep good leaders awake at night. Terry takes you from the surreal to the real world of strategic thinking and planning."

– James Whalen, Vice President, DirecTV, Inc

"Hits the nail on the head with fresh approaches to design and implement projects that achieve their goals."

– Philippe Goetschel, Director (Retired), Microsoft Corporation

"Lots of management tools sound good in theory but are hard to apply. Terry provides a practical planning breakthrough that has helped our team to start faster, think smarter and get more done."

– Lynn Ballard, IT Security Manager, Beckman Coulter

"This book provides concise, simple, and highly effective tools to turn problems into action plans. No project is too complex when broken down using Terry's four strategic questions and the Logical Framework tool."

– Anne Wu, Lean Six Sigma Black Belt, 3M Unitek

"You changed how I do my planning and this has significantly increased my ability to reach my goals."

– Laurie Triplett, Environmental Physicist, Los Alamos National Laboratory

"Turn Strategy Into Action demystifies the art of converting a fuzzy problem into an action plan. Definitely "simple" without being "simplistic."

– Noel Ellis, Chief Process Engineer, Raytheon

"We use your breakthrough methods to nail down our business strategies and to avoid the preventable pitfalls of execution."

– Wolfgang Royer, General Manager Customer Service Central Europe, Middle East & Africa, Sony Ericsson Mobile Communications AB

"These are effective management tools that can translate strategic plans into projects that deliver."

– Elaine Khoo, Manager, Design Singapore Council

"These tools will not only benefit you, but will benefit your whole team."

– Kumar Talinki, Senior Software Engineer, Symantec Corporation

"Makes it much easier to visualize complex and large projects. This helps you to effectively communicate and present your ideas to the whole team."

– Keith Bonnici, Program Manager, Tekes, Finnish Funding Agency for Technology & Innovation

"I put your creative and flexible system to work and got results right away. Thanks for the insights."

– Gary G. Lo, Regional Finance & Information Management Director Johnson & Johnson Vision Care, Asia Pacific Division

"Terry is one of the best project practitioners I know. His methods are fresh, powerful, and effective. You are wise to read this book if you want to avoid the pitfalls that doom many critical projects."

– George Morrisey, Author, Morrisey on Planning series

"If a road map's worth is measured not solely by your arrival, but also the confidence by which you travel, then this is a priceless map to organizational success. Using this has unleashed motivation and generated company-wide optimism that surpassed our expectations. This is one road map you should not travel without."

– David Skinner, President, Holiday Group

"Terry brings his dynamic presentation style to an innovative project planning book that makes a traditionally boring but critical subject come alive."

– Donald S. Remer, PhD, PE
Oliver C. Field, Professor of Engineering, Harvey Mudd College

"This approach gave our planners, managers and analysts the tools and insight to successfully redirect a major process reengineering effort taking place in a rapidly changing IT landscape."

– Michael J. Greenhalgh, Supervisor, Sacramento Municipal Utility District

"Strategic management can be a very dry subject. However, true masters can turn this dry topic into a most enlightening and highly usable management tool. Terry is one such rare master. You would be wise to read his book and even wiser to attend his course."

Regent B.H. Khor, Senior Marketing Officer,
JTC Corporation, Government of Singapore

"Finally! A tool that makes absolute sense. I was immediately able to apply this Logical Framework to an existing project that needed clarity and organization."

– Charalynn Macedo, IT Group Leader,
(Technology Research Organization)

To Mom and Dad,
who taught me the value
of taking action,
and to my sweetheart.

Table of Contents

Acknowledgements

Many people along my career journey have helped me to master the art and science of designing and leading strategic projects. Thanks to Leon Rosenberg, the visionary behind this process, as well as to Molly Hageboeck and Larry Posner, my colleagues at a Washington, D.C. consulting firm where these concepts blossomed. Long conversations with Merlyn Kettering, Marcus Ingle, Larry Cooley, and Moses Thompson deepened my understanding of strategic concepts.

When UCLA Extension invited me to teach in its esteemed Technical Management Program two decades ago, I adapted these concepts to business technology and research environments. Thanks to UCLA's Dr. Bill Goodin, Dr. Frank Burris, and Joon Lee, for their ongoing support.

Steve Haines and colleagues at the Haines Centre for Strategic Management have provided a stimulating forum for linking these tools to business excellence.

John Assaraf, Alan Weiss, Bill Gower, Dr. Hendrie Weisinger, and Dr. Keith Russell, provided encouraging words just when I needed them. Kerry Dean Hooper helped breathe life into dull paragraphs. Shari Fowler caught the glitches and used her "magic" to create smoother, more intelligible writing.

My greatest thanks goes to the many clients I have been privileged to serve. By rolling up our sleeves and solving real problems together, we proved that these concepts work, and add value in complex environments.

This manuscript would still be piles of scribbled mush without Somrutai (Maiky) Binhason, who typed my endless stream of massive revisions without complaint. I couldn't have done it without her and the rest of my team, especially Missy Adams, Sastrawut Panaree, Mike Kent, and Sinee Angel.

A cracker-jack review team put great energy into critiquing early manuscript drafts. Thank you David Giramma, Pamm St. John, Rob Farrington, Deanna Deeds, Brian Cracchiola, Walter Grassl, Jamie Truong, Naomi Becker, Benjamin Grover, Robert Martinez, Eugene Garrilov, Gerald Turner, Dean Sanderpoint and Kazumi Tait. Your feedback made this a much better book.

My three superdogs – Bingo the pound-hound, Mushka the shy ShitZu, and Chico the lion-hearted Maltese – snuggled under my desk and kept me company during the many long nights of writing, rewriting, polishing, and completing.

This book was a long labor of love that would not have been completed without the incredible support of my entire team. Thanks to you all!

Introduction

If your work requires more brains than brawn, you need this book. You and I are among the growing army of knowledge workers and professionals who must deliver results in an increasingly fast-paced, demanding, competitive world. This book provides powerful, easy-to-use planning and implementation tools to accomplish your ambitious agendas.

Today's professionals must be multi-skilled, and quick to learn new technologies as they emerge. Expertise in your own profession is not enough. That's because the most critical strategies and projects involve different technical disciplines, organizational elements, and stakeholder interests. To triumph in today's competitive arena, you must also be a *Strategic Project Manager,* with a skill-set and mind-set to handle the challenges of a complex world .

By mastering the discipline of Strategic Project Management, you will multiply your ability to execute the new ideas your organization needs to thrive, as well as advance your own career.

I wrote this book because I've seen far too many educated, experienced, and talented people fail to get the results they want for lack of the right tools to think, plan, and act in a strategic way. The system you will be reading about fills this void and will give you the edge you need.

Applying the ideas in this book will multiply your strategic effectiveness, whether you are already a seasoned pro, a beginner, or somewhere in between. CEOs and executives will find this as valuable as supervisors, scientists, engineers, entrepreneurs, mid-level managers, project leaders, team members, generalists, and specialists of all types. Wild-eyed visionaries, dreamers and entrepreneurs can use this step-by-step, flexible approach to develop sound action plans for critical projects and change initiatives more rapidly and effectively than with any other method.

Regardless of your background, occupation, or position, you'll discover a powerful way to tackle just about any issue that crosses your path. The bottom line: you and your team can jump-start complex projects smoothly and achieve impressive results sooner.

My Lifelong Project Love Affair

During my 35-year career, I've helped thousands of teams worldwide get ambitious projects off the ground. These projects have ranged from setting up education systems in Bangladesh to helping American scientists design surveillance systems for detecting nuclear tests by rogue nations. They've included programs to strengthen security in financial institutions, grow new enterprises to the next level, increase agricultural productivity in developing countries, consolidate IT systems after mergers, improve the ways correctional institutions handle prisoners, and help governmental agencies streamline their service delivery.

These projects have taken place in high and low tech environments, in Fortune 500 companies, small firms, state and federal government agencies, research laboratories, and academic institutions.

Many different experiences over time contributed to my passion for strategic thinking and projects, an interest that started long before my professional career.

My lifelong love affair with projects began at age six when I was playing in the sandbox with a garden hose. After crafting a small sand mountain in mid-box, I stuck the hose into the sand hill to bring out a small river of water, which I would quickly redirect here and there in its downhill rush, avoiding the hazardous patch where the cat liked to scratch.

My goal was to build the largest possible dam, until the water would eventually overflow and exit through a knothole in the pine planks surrounding the sandbox. Each time I'd try a different approach, adding channels to guide the water, using action-learning to improve the strategy long before knowing what that term even meant. Sometimes my buddy Murray would help. When lunchtime came, we'd tromp into the house – victorious, but wet and sandy, much to Mom's chagrin.

My passion for technology began in eighth grade, when I built a small rocket and "launched guppies into inner space," as Rocket News later described it. The national press buzz which followed my sending a pregnant guppy and her slim companion a thousand feet in the air inspired me to pursue aerospace engineering at the University of Washington. It's amazing how one pivotal experience can launch an entire career.

In high school I was too small to play football in high school and too shy to date girls, so I played chess. Chess has one clear goal: capture the opposing king to win the game.

Chess is a marvelous way to learn business strategy because it encourages "down-board thinking" and mental flexibility. Chess forces you to think about the future implications of current moves and to explore "what if" scenarios before each decision. One must also pay attention to the shifting environment of the game board, and make informed *Assumptions* about what is likely to unfold.

While in college I worked at Boeing, part-time, playing a minor role in the roll-out of the very first 747. A summer internship with NASA found me devouring all the program management books in Center's library and meeting with my hero, Dr. Wernher von Braun, the visionary leader who led the U.S. lunar landing program. Dr. von Braun seemed both intrigued and amused by my rocket-fish experiments.

After getting an MBA at Harvard, I landed a program management position in the Office of the Secretary of Transportation, in Washington DC, where we coordinated program planning for federal transportation agencies.

Following my stint as a Fed, I switched careers and became an international development consultant. At a management consulting company called PCI, I learned a tool for managing difficult projects. My job was to teach this tool to managers and train project teams in countries like Bangladesh, Thailand, Indonesia, Pakistan, Senegal, and the Ivory Coast.

After starting my own consulting company, my client base shifted to corporations, government agencies, and research institutions. These clients were very different from my earlier developing country clients, but much to my surprise, they faced very similar issues – organizing across boundaries, building strong teams, sorting out complexity, and managing key success factors.

Even more surprising, I found that the same project management tool which worked so well in developing countries was amazingly well-suited for handling the complex tangle of issues my new clients faced.

Recently I've begun providing clients a unique approach to planning and change in association with the Haines Centre for Strategic Management. The process covered in this book energizes strategic Goals and turns them into action.

This book completes a decade-long writing effort and contributes to my life mission, which is to share the very best strategic management practices with motivated men and women who aspire to make a positive difference in all dimensions of their work and their lives.

Getting the Most from this Book

Turn Strategy Into Action takes a big picture holistic view that is usually missing in project management. These concepts will help you to:

- Convert any problem, idea, or opportunity into clear action plans.

- Identify key project Objectives and sharpen the logic of your strategy.

- Link your effort to the larger strategic Goals.

- Uncover and deal with the hidden Assumptions and probable pitfalls that can derail your efforts.

- Reduce risk in advance, and thus avoid the primary causes of project failure.

- Communicate concisely and build support of champions and stakeholders.

- Organize cross-functional task forces and other diverse groups into committed and effective teams that are clear about who needs to do what, when, and how.

This book is organized into three logical parts.

The three chapters of Part One explore the principles that make Strategic Project Management so effective. Chapter One describes what makes this approach unique and points out mistakes to avoid. Chapter Two introduces the four critical strategic questions, *if-then* thinking, and the art of formulating hypotheses. Chapter Three unveils what may be the world's best kept management secret, the Logical Framework.

Building on that foundation of understanding, the four chapters of Part Two offer step-by-step instructions for how to design executable projects by answering the four critical strategic questions. Chapter Four covers the fine points of defining and aligning Objectives, while Chapter Five tackles measurement issues. Chapter Six demonstrates how to reduce problems in advance by managing Assumptions, while Chapter Seven covers detailed work planning.

Part Three puts it all together in three chapters. Chapter Eight explores the human dynamics of projects. Chapter Nine discusses the art of action-learning and execution, while Chapter Ten describes a dozen ways to implement these ideas, and provides tips for getting started.

You'll discover many client case studies, project examples, and key point summaries at the end of each chapter. The appendix contains practical checklists, a glossary of terms, a half-dozen best-practice examples, free articles, and other helpful resources.

Along the way, you'll witness how some of my clients have put these tools into action. While all the examples are real, some have been edited for confidentiality, abbreviated to fit the space, or modified to highlight key learning points. For readers who want the details, you will find downloadable versions of these and other examples at *www.ManagementPro.com*.

At the risk of annoying English teachers worldwide, certain strategic management words have been capitalized, even in mid-sentence. These terms have been given precise definitions and have been capitalized to emphasize the explicit use of those terms.

For a greater range of examples, see the companion book *Strategic Project Management Solutions Handbook*. This collection of 53 real-world applications covers projects in marketing, strategic planning, process improvement, information technology, research and development, professional growth, and other topics.

The best way to master these materials is to read this book at least twice. The first time, simply aim to understand how the concepts fit together. On your second time through, apply the tips at the end of each chapter to your own issues. These ideas are meaty, so don't hesitate to underline key sentences and scribble in the margins.

Strategic Project Management helps you think smarter, move faster, and accomplish ambitious objectives more quickly. People who can do that are a rare breed. You are about to become one of them.

Part One:
Are You Strategic?

These three chapters examine the power of Strategic Project Management and introduce the simple two-word principle that is the heart of
strategic thinking. Then you'll learn the four critical strategic questions,
and will be invited to "join my workshop" to learn about the Logical
Framework – a flexible tool that handles issues of all types and sizes.

Chapter 1: Avoiding the Deadly Planning Mistakes

"Knowing is not enough, we must apply.
Willing is not enough, we must do."

– Johann Wolfgang von Goethe

Tackling the Big Hairy Issues

My clients are my best teachers. I've been fortunate to consult with interesting men and women all around the world – many facing every kind of issue you can imagine. All of them have been accomplished professionals doing important and non-routine work.

I'd like you to meet some of my favorites. Their challenges appear very different, but from a broader perspective, there are some common overarching themes. Can you spot them?

- A global nonprofit health organization needs to create an enterprise management system serving very diverse users worldwide.

- A Middle East sheik needs to "win the peace" after "winning the war" against foreign-financed insurgents.

- A scientific research team needs to secure funding needed to develop advanced airborne chemical agent detectors.

- A pioneering web-based timeshare resale company chooses to reinvent itself to handle fierce new competition.

- A nuclear engineer must organize technical experts from several national research laboratories to create a plan to recover radioactive materials that could be diverted to make dirty bombs.

- The director of a social service agency caring for mentally and physically handicapped residents must solve the root cause of mysterious injuries to their residents.

- A small but innovative company, which manufactures sophisticated, portable optical-electric equipment must ramp up to handle explosive growth.

- A Singapore government ministry aims to attract multi-national companies to locate their headquarters there.

What's common? Each organization faced a unique and difficult situation involving multiple players and tricky issues. Success required managing unpredictable political and organizational variables in addition to technical and cost factors. In most cases, the best path to the goal was not apparent from the start, and a solution had to be created and skillfully implemented.

To be successful, all needed a ***strategic approach***, not the tactical task/schedule focus which dominates traditional project management techniques.

I'm willing to bet that your work involves planning or executing important, non-routine projects of one type or another. My hunch is that the issues you are involved with include one or more of these dynamics:

- **Hard to measure.** Can't easily kick the tires to track progress.
- **High stakes**. Important to the organization.
- **Complex.** Can't always see a clear solution path at the start; must learn by doing.
- **Consequential**. Success brings benefits, failure brings pain.
- **Ad hoc team**. May require new players coming together as a team.
- **Time pressure**. You need to move fast.
- **Multiple stakeholders**. Involves and impacts many parties.
- **Risky**. You can't control all the variables that the solution requires.
- **Visible**. People who count are watching and keeping score.

How many of these sound familiar? If more than one of these rings true for you, this book will benefit you immensely.

Based on hundreds of consulting projects done around the world, I've sharpened a planning process that addresses the tough issues, opportunities, and problems on your plate. The process you are about to discover will give you the insights you've always needed and sensed were missing from other approaches.

Mastering Strategic Project Management

Today, all people deal with projects in one way or another, whether as sponsors, team members, project managers, or stakeholders. Your job title may not read **Project Manager**, but you would be wise to learn to think like one.

Like it or not, being well-educated, competent, and hard working is not enough to enjoy professional success, career advancement and personal satisfaction in today's world. Expertise in your own professional area is *necessary,* but not *sufficient*. Being good at what you do is a must, but by itself, it's not enough.

For example, to create a new product, having an idea is *necessary*, but the idea alone is *not sufficient* to get the product on the shelves. In fact, the world is full of good ideas, but only a few ever make it beyond the realm of wishful thinking. Later you'll see how the concept of *necessary and sufficient conditions* sharpens your project strategy.

Project management has become a must-have skill for everyone. That's because the most critical work gets done through team-centered projects which often cut across different technical disciplines, organizational perspectives, and stakeholder interests. By project management skills, I don't mean just knowing how to draw a Gantt chart or develop a work breakdown structure. These project management basics aren't enough unless they are front-loaded with a strategic thinking process of some sort to design and develop the *right* projects.

Why Read This Book?

If you are new to project management, or find yourself suddenly assigned project responsibility without having formal training, the concepts in this book will give you a solid organizing framework. If you are a seasoned pro or certified project manager, this book offers you the missing big picture piece that distinguishes visionary project mangers from the rest of the crowd. Sponsors and champions will find a methodology to concisely communicate their strategic intent to those responsible for delivery. Team leaders will discover a fresh way to pull together cross functional teams. Individual contributors will learn tips to be more effective on their chunk of the project pie. The bottom line is this: whatever role you play, this strategic approach offers concepts and tools to multiply what you can accomplish by changing how you think, plan, and act.

Seeing Projects in a New Light

While projects have been around since the Pharaohs built the pyramids, today's projects deserve a fresh definition. The classic definition of project – *an organized set of activities to achieve specific objectives, on time and within budget* – still holds true, but projects are much more than this.

Projects are engines of change: organizing frameworks for executing strategic initiatives, and people-powered performance machines designed to achieve worthy objectives.

The new breed of projects we face are not easy to pull off. These are not our parents' projects, with clear goals and simple organization structures in stable environments. Many require managing the intangibles of information, behaviors, and processes. Very few projects today follow a straight path, with clear solutions that are obvious from the beginning, and mapable from start to finish. Most follow curved paths, demanding iteration and ongoing learning. Typically, we must draw our own maps while driving toward the destination in an ongoing process of learning and discovery.

The most potent opportunities seldom show up labeled as "projects," but arrive disguised as problems, issues, or murky messes. Tackling so-called B-HAGS (Big, Hairy, Audacious Goals), as Jim Collins describes them in *Built to Last*, involves juggling a full spectrum of slippery objectives which can be difficult to define, let alone manage.

Good Strategy Is Not Enough

Companies of every size and type, striving to deliver exceptional customer value, need the right strategies. But smart strategy is only a ticket for general admission, not for a front row seat. *Fortune Magazine* reports that 75% of all strategies fail. In Information Technology, the statistics are even more dismal. Why such a bleak track record? The problem is usually not a lack of good strategies, but a failure to execute them effectively.

My premise is that this "execution gap" occurs, in part, because of the ineffective and inefficient way we design projects. Strategies tell us where to go, but only projects will get us there. The ability to turn good ideas into well-designed, actionable, projects is a potent competitive advantage, and the keys to doing that are found at the heart of this book.

What's Coming Up

I'll walk you through a flexible thinking process, and give you the tools to sort through the fog of fuzzy ideas, develop sound strategies, and turn them into executable plans. You'll appreciate how these tools scale up and down to handle issues of any size and flex to fit multiple situations you may face. But first, let's review why most project plans are inadequate. See how many of these resonate with your personal experience.

Beware These Six Deadly Planning Mistakes

I must admit that not all of the projects I've worked with were roaring successes. Some were total disasters. Reflecting back, I've learned this key lesson: *more often than not, the seeds of success or failure are planted during the early planning and team building stage.*

Virtually every failed project suffered from one or more of the following six deadly planning mistakes. They are not listed in any particular order of priority, but indeed, they often travel together like a nasty pack of snarling junkyard dogs.

1. Tolerating Vague Objectives

"We don't know where we are going, but at least we're making good time!"

Projects run this way usually end up going nowhere. In the rush to implement, too little serious, up-front thinking goes into clarifying Objectives, Measures, and their interconnections. While Objectives may start off vague, there is no excuse for letting them remain that way. Left fuzzy and immeasurable, vague Objectives invite finger-pointing, blame, and predictable failure. Chapters Four and Five offer practical tools to define, measure, and organize your Objectives.

2. Ignoring Environmental Context

"What we don't know won't hurt us."

Well, it just might. Projects unfold in unpredictable ways, but people often think myopically and ignore how risk factors outside their project boundaries affect them. While you can't control the wind, you can adjust your sails. You can examine which externalities might impact your efforts and prepare accordingly.

Chapter Six shows how to examine environmental influences, and then turns them into *Assumptions* that must be true for your project to work. Assumptions can be tested for probability and impact to reduce risk. This doesn't guarantee success, but it sure ups the odds.

3. Poor Planning Tools and Process

"This project management software can handle all our planning needs."

When your only tool is a hammer, the whole world looks like a nail. While I have healthy respect for project software such as Microsoft Project™ and Primavera™, these programs become downright dangerous when used too early in the process because they create a false sense of certainty.

Making a task list or booting up project management software isn't the place to start, despite how many people do just that. Don't get me wrong – you need these tools, but they are best used when it comes time to start breaking down tasks, not when you are still firming up Objectives. Before firing up your PC, flesh out your project strategy using the thinking system detailed in this book.

Turn Strategy Into Action teaches a proven process to sharpen Goals and strategies. After you put these higher Objectives in place, but *only after*, Chapter Seven guides you in using software to spell out detailed work plans.

4. Neglecting Stakeholder Interests

"I see no reason why anyone wouldn't support this."
"Everyone involved with or affected by this project supports it."

Ever notice how everyone involved in or affected by the project seems to have their own agenda? Projects are real-life dramas played out by multiple actors who bring varying degrees of interest and support. Projects suffer without stakeholder cooperation and participation.

Stephen Haines, a leading systems thinker, said it best: "People support what they help create." Early stakeholder involvement increases buy-in, reduces resistance, and paves the way for smooth implementation. Stakeholder involvement doesn't mean you can always please everyone, or that you even need to try. You may choose to ignore, compromise, trade, apply pressure, or find other ways to deal with some people. Chapter Eight offers a stakeholder analysis tool that will help you bring key players into your planning process.

5. One Shot Planning

"We're too busy doing to keep planning."

Like home-baked bread that grows moldy with time, plans have a limited shelf-life. They are only as good as the information available when the plan was created. Over time, as conditions change, project plans should be updated to reflect new learning and progress.

Updating goes beyond monitoring costs and fine-tuning schedules. Updating means periodically stepping back and examining how the environment has changed and revising strategies as needed. The "Be Cycle-Logical" principle in Chapter Nine describes how to keep your strategies fresh via iterative planning, implementation, and evaluation, followed by re-planning in an ongoing project management cycle..

6. Mismanaging Team Dynamics

"Of course my team will perform – they've been assigned to this project."

Project success requires the committed, coordinated action of many people. While some project managers run rough shod over their team, others make it a positive growth experience. Tap into human dynamics. Find a way, using tips in Chapter Eight, to make your project a win for everyone, and you will have a sure-fire team.

Consider Your Own Experience

Think about the disappointing projects you have encountered. Did they suffer some of these same serious mistakes? Looking back with 20-20 hindsight, could more heads-up and deliberate planning have improved the results? Think also about the winners you've driven to the finish line. What was different? Did your successful projects manage to avoid these common mistakes?

While I can't guarantee you 100% success in the future, I can promise that you will put the odds in your favor by using the strategies and street-smart wisdom in the pages that follow.

Here's a quick preview of the solution concepts covered in the pages ahead, and how they address the six planning mistakes.

Planning Mistakes	Solution Concepts
1. Tolerating Vague Objectives	• Make objectives clear and measurable • Identify logical levels and *if-then* links • Define your strategic hypotheses • Define *why* before *what* and *how*
2. Ignoring Environmental Context	• Scan the environment for influence factors • Understand internal and external context • Identify risk elements • Make, test, manage and monitor assumptions
3. Poor Planning Process	• Choose common planning model and language • Plan top down, test bottom-up • Plan for the plan • Use the Logical Framework as a central planning tool
4. Neglecting Stakeholder Interests	• Remember – people support what they help create • Involve people who matter • Understand others' perspectives • Build consensus and commitment
5. One Shot Planning	• Treat project documents as living plans, organic in nature • Be "cycle logical"- plan, implement, evaluate, and replan • Iterate and update in pre-determined action cycles • Constantly refine the strategic hypothesis
6. Mismanaging Team Dynamics	• Build-in payoffs (fun, learning, rewards) • Grow the team while growing the plan • Sharpen the who-when-what-how • Manage with emotional intelligence

Chapter Key Points

1. Every competent professional who masters the Strategic Project Management mindset and skillset gains a competitive edge that most people lack. With them, you can tackle just about any issue that crosses your path.

2. Fast moving environments call for smarter, more flexible ways of thinking. Traditional project management tools are limiting because they focus on activity, budget and schedule. Strategic Project Management tools fill the gap by emphasizing Goals, Measures, and risk.

3. Many worthy projects are doomed from the start because of deadly planning mistakes. Use the tools ahead to ward off these goal-stoppers.

4. Empowering yourself with these mental power-tools sets you above all those who are still trying to fit round problems into square solutions!

Chapter 2: Building Strong Project Backbones

"If one link is broken, the entire chain is broken"

– Yiddish Proverb

Asking the Four Critical Strategic Questions

The call came from Keith, an engineer who had attended one of my executive strategy workshops at UCLA. Keith worked in a well-known company that needed to launch a critical initiative, but their task force had made little progress after several frustrating meetings. Keith invited me to facilitate their next discussion, attended by a cross-section of company personnel with heavy representation from the Information Technology Department.

The dozen key players in the conference room looked frustrated when I entered. I listened to a lively technical discussion on the merits of Linux versus Windows, C++ versus Ajax/Java evaluations, and stuff I had no clue about. They were well into the *how* of the project, without being clear on the *what* and *why*. Then a bald, geeky executive glared at me and asked, "Okay, you're the consultant. We seem to be stuck – what should we do?"

My consulting approach helps clients think more systematically so they can develop great solutions. All great solutions begin by asking the right questions. The following carefully-crafted questions work wonders in virtually any situation. There are four Critical Strategic Questions:

1. What are we trying to accomplish and why?

I responded to the executive by tossing out that question. He and his team looked at each other as if to say, "for the money we are paying this guy, we expect a brilliant answer, not a simple question." While hardly profound, this fundamental question is the perfect place to start – whatever your issue.

Surprisingly, the motivating Objectives behind projects are not always clear, or are badly communicated in a corporate memo or vague strategic plan. Sometimes this question gets answered superficially in a catch phrase early in the game, but is not revisited, reconsidered, and revalidated until later.

The question of *what* the project should accomplish, and more importantly, *why* it needs to be done, deserves fine-tuned attention because those answers drive everything else. In the rush to decide on the *how*, *who*, and *when* of a project, people often gloss over the *why*.

This question posed to Keith's team cut through clouds of confusion and numerous answers tumbled out, which I captured on the white board. The discussion rapidly shifted from technical solutions to customer needs and expectations, as well as the operational benefits expected. Later, they would organize these Objectives into a logical sequence.

Professionals today are often told **what** needs to be done, but are not really clear on **why** it is needed. Thus, it's very easy to become lost in the technical jungle of **how.** People first need to know the higher level Objectives that answer the whole "what are we trying to accomplish and why?" question in order to spark intrinsic motivation and unleash their full-spectrum brain power.

When Keith's team reached agreement on several Objectives, I asked this next question.

2. How will we measure success?

Their facial expressions suggested that I had revealed some magic formula that unlocks the universe. This question is significant because Measures flesh out and anchor what the Objectives really mean.

This question seldom gets the attention it deserves, in part due to the false belief that the answer must be obvious, or else senior management (or whoever) wouldn't have mandated the project. One of Keith's team members provided a perfect example when he replied, "They said that our Goal is to deliver customer value, so isn't it clear what constitutes success?"

It's easy to presume that accountants, analysts, or "some other department" will decide whether or not the project is successful, so tackling the question may seem to be irrelevant or a waste of time. However, until you define how success will be measured, even the most sincere visions are no more than high-falutin' fluff. As we sketched out clear Success Measures for each Objective, the mood in the room changed. The team felt a sense of progress that had been missing from earlier sessions. Now they were rolling along the right path and the worry lines on Keith's brow softened.

3. What other conditions must exist?

When I posed this question, the geeky executive who had glared at me earlier smiled. This question puts your project, issue, or initiative into a larger strategic context. Asking this expands the dimensions of thinking to include some of the outside factors you are relying on, which may disrupt your carefully crafted plans. Capable, responsible professionals conscientiously focus, all too often, on areas they *can* affect or control because it's seemingly irresponsible or inappropriate to worry (on the client's dime, no less) about things they *can't* control. Asking this question also gives permission to think outside the direct project scope boundaries and situate the project into its larger, often murky context.

I jotted down key *Assumptions* about other factors which influenced or affected their efforts. They began sharing their concerns about how to provide necessary training, how this system would mesh with processes already in place, how to ensure sufficient resources and other critical issues that could easily have been missed. Later, we tested the validity of these Assumptions to discover potential risk areas and to reduce problems in advance. With that in place, the last question could be answered with greater confidence.

4. How do we get there?

Now, but not before, was the time to address the nitty-gritty details. At this point, project management software is helpful to begin detailing the work plan.

The majority of project teams I have witnessed tend to dive deep into a task and schedule analysis much too soon, or they get sidelined by premature technical arguments. They gloss over the first three questions in a rush to get moving. By ignoring or short-changing earlier questions, their neatly printed project plans are like lipstick on a pig – lovely at first glance, but masking some seriously ugly flaws underneath. The value of this fourth question comes from consciously placing it in its only, truly functional place in the planning sequence: last.

These four Critical Strategic Questions form the heart of Strategic Project Management. Each needs to be asked and answered, in exactly this order. Of course, the questions are iterative and interconnected. It's smart to give first-cut answers and cycle through them again and again, each time sharpening your thinking and improving your confidence in the strategy. In the next chapter, you'll learn a simple strategic thinking tool, called the Logical Framework, that elegantly organizes your answers to these questions.

The Two Missing Words in Strategy

Execute an online search at Amazon or Barnes & Noble for "strategy books" and you'll find over 10,000 different publications. Various authors address strategy issues with concepts like visioning, goals, positioning, niching, core competencies, and so on. But most gloss over the essential strategy issue that you, as an executive, professional, or "accidental project manager," must face. Sure, defining the right Goals and strategies is important, but after this is pinned down, the essential question becomes, "*How* can you make it happen?"

The answer to that question constitutes the art and science of *Turning Strategy into Action*. Fortunately, the essence of the answer can be boiled down into two simple words: *if* and *then*.

Diamonds in the Cornfield

In the movie *Field of Dreams*, Kevin Costner's character contemplates building a baseball park in the middle of an Iowa cornfield. He says to himself:

"*If* we build it, *Then* they will come."

These words capture a strategic principle that is both simple and profound: *if-then* thinking. Understanding and applying this basic principle will leverage your ability to produce project payoffs.

If-then thinking is also called "cause-effect" or "means-ends" thinking, and it's a natural thinking process that powers your mental models when you plan. Planning is nothing more than imagining some future desired conditions, and then thinking backwards about the cause and effect steps needed to get there.

If-then offers a strategic management language that lets you think top-down and backwards from future goals, as well as think bottom-up and forward from the present, thus creating solid bridges between current reality and future dreams. This phrase also illustrates the power of human vision and commitment, two ever-necessary competencies not to be set aside lightly.

Linking two Objectives into a logical *if-then* relationship forms a *hypothesis*, a predictive statement of cause and effect that involves uncertainty. In plain language, a hypothesis is an educated guess that reflects our experience and best guess prediction of how the world (or at least the project at hand) works.

Stringing multiple *if-then* linkages together forms multi-level *strategic hypotheses*, a logic stream based on the generic formula "*if* A *then* B; *if* B *then* C, *if* C *then* D." Every project builds around presumed strategic hypotheses, whether or not they are consciously defined. When these hypotheses are fuzzy, when causal linkages are unclear, undefined or illogical, your plan is a crap shoot. The learnable discipline of *if-then* thinking can dramatically boost your odds of success because it forces rigorous systematic thought.

Reverse Your Reading Direction

We are taught to read from the top of a page to the bottom, but in the diagrams which follow, it works best to read from bottom to top. It seems counter-intuitive at first, but you'll soon get comfortable with reading *if-then* hypotheses bottom-up.

You can diagram this basic "*if* we build it, *then* they will come" linkage as follows. Remember to start at the bottom and read up.

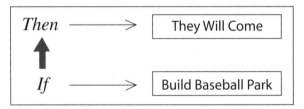

Here are several examples of *if-then* logic, visually displayed as linked hypotheses. Remember, start at the bottom and work up, connecting the phrases together with *if-then* logic. Let's walk through the logic of the first example.

"*If* we organize a block watch program, *then* we can reduce crime; *if* we reduce crime, *then* we will have better neighborhoods."

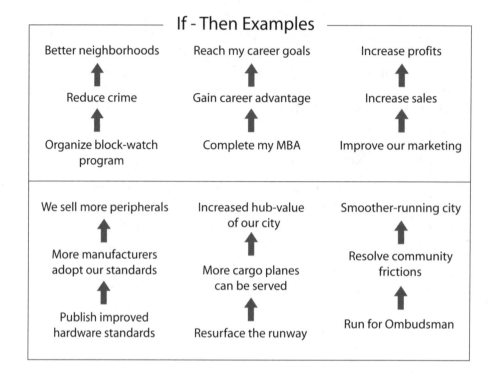

Some strategic hypotheses are simple, i.e., "*If* I get married, *then* I'll be happy." But usually, they are more complicated and comprised of connective tissue of multiple links, i.e., "*If* we launch this new product quickly, *then* we'll discourage competitors; *if* we discourage competitors, *then* we'll increase market share; *if* we increase market share, *then* we'll dominate the industry."

As you read them from the bottom up, focus on the *if-then* logic linking each pair of Objectives. Notice how the higher Objectives tend to be global, general, and influenced by many factors other than our project. We normally design projects top down, beginning with Objectives at the top and working down, but mentally test the logic – and implement – by working bottom up.

Making Strategy Simple

The essence of strategy – how to get to where you want to be – is embedded directly into *if-then* statements, much like the chocolaty goodness baked into mom's hot-from-the-oven cookies. The execution of any corporate or project strategy can be expressed using *if-then* logic to connect related

Objectives. *If-then* is a neutral language that crosses disciplinary boundaries, allowing engineers, accountants, and CEOs to share the same view of the world. This viewpoint is enormously helpful because the various players of diverse backgrounds can compare and integrate their mental models, and thus develop an informed and superior approach.

Think of projects as carefully structured experiments. During project design, you form a set of hypotheses presumed to be true; implementation tests the validity of those hypotheses. This perspective lets you manage in a way that's scientific and strategic, as well as street-smart.

Why am I stressing the importance of *if-then* thinking? Because most project teams miss this crucial concept entirely. Project plans may turn into dozens of pages of tasks, but if you can't describe, with simple *if-then* language, how your good efforts ripple up to impact important organization Goals, you aren't able to optimize the benefits you aim to deliver. It's hard to *achieve* what you can't *explain*.

Key Distinction

If-then causal logic may seem obvious, but there is a twist: causal logic is different from sequential logic. Here's the critical distinction: In sequential logic, A precedes B in time. A must happen before B, although it does not cause B. But with causal logic, A not only precedes B, *A causes B to happen*.

When building a baseball park in Iowa, sequential logic can identify the logical order of action steps: cut the corn, plow the field, plant grass, etc. It's true that "*if* we cut the corn, *then* we can level the surface," but such a statement expresses a time-based sequential relationship – do this before you do that. Cutting the corn does not cause the surface to level itself; it simply precedes it in time. Gantt charts and network diagrams do a good job of showing sequential task logic and dependencies, but they seldom show causal logic.

Sequential logic, however, is not strategic. Hunkering down and completing all the tasks on a Gantt chart doesn't necessarily get you to the Goal. Many great ballparks, flashy products, and new processes have been built that remain largely unused, unneeded, or unwanted.

Being more precise, we have to admit that building a ballpark, stadium, or golf course does not, in itself, cause people to come. Having a winning team, creating successful promotions, and providing easy access are all factors that directly impact the strategic hypothesis. At the same time, it's true that 'they can't come' unless and until 'it's built.' So, building the ballpark is a necessary prerequisite to people coming, but it is not sufficient, in and of itself, to *cause* them to come.

Observe, too, that the hope "they will come" is still a hypothesis, a deeply-desired view of how the world will respond to the project. Wrapped in that hope is the conviction, the desire, that *if* we build it, **then** they will come. This hope makes the heart of the movie beat, but if you allow conviction to substitute for rigorous cause-effect reasoning, you're in trouble.

But why does Costner's character want them to come? What's the bigger Objective behind this project? Costner's character was behind on mortgage payments and slipping into foreclosure, so we can infer that "save the farm" was his higher Objective. Let's extend the *if-then* linkages up a level, as well as down a level, to identify the steps necessary to build the park.

Our logic chain now looks like this:

Reading up from the bottom…

▶ *If* we design the park, get equipment, etc.

  ▶ *Then* we can build a baseball park,

▶ *If* we build a baseball park,

  ▶ *Then* they will come,

▶ *If* they come (and pay),

  ▶ *Then* we can save the farm.

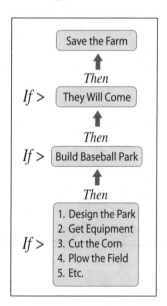

We've now constructed a four level strategic hypothesis, the logical backbone of any project. Note how the linkages start with do-able tasks at the bottom and percolate up to high-level Goals.

This simple notion of *if-then* thinking is the secret to successful design and implementation of strategies, projects, and action initiatives of all types. Project design establishes a set of hypotheses, or educated guesses, believed to be true. Implementation determines the real-world validity of those hypotheses. With this viewpoint, you can consider projects to be structured scientific experiments.

You may not win the Nobel Prize, but the quality of your thinking will be worthy of gold medals.

Test Your Strategic If-Then IQ

Brainstorming to generate answers to the first strategic question – *what are we trying to accomplish and why?* – produces a list of possible Objectives, but they are not in any particular order. You then need to convert this scrambled list into a logically ordered list. An example:

Scrambled Objectives	Organized Objectives
Get great product idea	Improve profits
	⬆
Market new product	Market new product
	⬆
Improve profits	Develop new product
	⬆
Develop new product	Get great product idea

Get the Idea?

Below are several sets of scrambled Objectives. Solve these examples to deepen your understanding of *if-then* logic. Start to unscramble by finding the "highest" Objective and putting it at the top. Stack the Objectives logically, top to bottom and bottom to top. You can start at the top and work down, or start from the bottom and work up, or work both ways. It's best to actually sketch them as shown in the example, with arrows and spaces between, or talk through them, mentally adding the linking *if-then* phrases.

Take a few minutes to work these examples, starting with a couple of light-hearted ones, and then moving on to the more serious ones. Check your answers at the end of this chapter.

Example #1:

- Get rich and move to Fiji
- Find a mate for Orville the hamster
- Breed prize hamsters
- Become "the hamster giant"

Example # 2:

- Meet lots of prospects
- Join an online dating service
- Find a soul mate
- Live happily ever after

Example #3:

- Design a new expense reporting system
- Reimburse employees faster
- Have happier employees
- Implement a new expense reporting system

Example #4:

- Identify ineffective practices
- Have staff use standard procedures
- Develop and publish best-practice procedures
- Improve corporate productivity

Example #5:

- Get promoted faster
- Get an MBA degree
- Become a CEO by age 40
- Take part-time classes

Example #6:

- Write and publish articles
- Become a sought-after industry expert
- Increase my professional reputation
- Identify needs in my field

Example #7:

- Increase corporate profit
- Develop a new product
- Increase corporate sales
- Market product successfully

Example #8:

- Develop portable land-mine detector
- Save lives and reclaim land
- Get research funding
- Deploy device in war-torn countries

Here's a final unscrambled example which shows an *illogical* strategic hypothesis – one with little probability of reaching the top of the *if-then* chain.

- Live a life of luxury

  ↑

- Win the lottery

  ↑

- Buy a lottery ticket

  ↑

- Drive to the 7-11

Note the virtual certainty of the lower-level *if-then* link. You can indeed drive to a 7-11 and buy a ticket. That much is guaranteed. But "*if* buy ticket, *then* win lottery" is a huge leap, with millions-to-one odds against you. As most lottery ticket buyers know, this *if-then* sequence strongly depends on random factors totally outside of your control.

Sorting Out Your Objectives

Let's dig deeper into the finer points about Objectives. The motivation driving all projects is simple: to achieve desired Objectives. Some examples:

- Develop a new management system
- Reduce time to market
- Produce new knowledge
- Invent the perfect gizmo
- Increase data security
- Generate increased profit
- Reengineer core processes

Yet defining Objectives is seldom straightforward because people interpret Objectives in very different ways based on their own technical background, thinking style, and vested interests. These inconsistent interpretations produce confusion and disappointment.

The very vocabulary used to describe Objectives adds to the confusion. Since no standard management vocabulary exists, people choose many different terms to express Objectives. Words like Goal, Purpose, aim, output, intention, Outcome, result, expectation, and vision are just a few examples. These terms may be perfectly clear to the person using them, or they may be thrown around without distinction, but their colleagues may have very different definitions.

(Let's agree to use the word *Objective* as a generic term to describe any and all project intentions, and get more precise in a few paragraphs.)

Complicating the picture, all projects have multiple Objectives, which exist at various "levels," ranging from short-term and specific, to long-term and general. Without a mechanism to clarify and logically organize Objectives, it's like the six blind men feeling an elephant; each perceives just one part and misses the logical whole. It's a wonder that *any* projects succeed!

The Secret of Clear Objectives

Crafting unambiguous and meaningful Objectives begins with the careful use of language. The key is to state them in a sentence using precise **verbs** and **descriptive phrases.** More about this in Chapter Four.

Link How You Think

It's surprising how seldom teams carefully define and examine the mental logic underpinning their efforts. That's dangerous. This oversight leads to projects that deliver end products, but fail to achieve business goals. Examples abound of new products developed which the market doesn't need, systems created which people don't use, and other well-intended, expensive projects which fail to leave a mark. You can avoid this disconnect by defining four levels of Objectives, defined as follows.

Goal — The high level "big picture" strategic or program Objective to which the project contributes. This is the "10,000 foot helicopter view" that provides an encompassing perspective.

Purpose — The impact we anticipate by doing the project; the expected changed conditions or result of producing Outcomes. We aim here, but can't fully control this level.

Outcomes — The specific results that the project team must deliver by managing Inputs.

Inputs — The activities we undertake and the resources necessary to produce Outcomes.

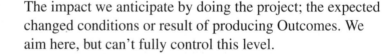

Read this "bottom-up" logic:

▶ *"If* we manage Inputs, *then* we can produce or deliver Outcomes;

▶ *If* we produce or deliver Outcomes, *then* we will achieve a Purpose;

▶ *If* we achieve a Purpose, *then* we contribute to an important Goal."

Or, expressed more succinctly:

▶ *"If* Inputs, *then* Outcomes;

▶ *If* Outcomes, *then* Purpose;

▶ *If* Purpose, *then* Goal."

The logic between levels is not random or accidental; each level forms a link in the strategic hypothesis. While the choice of words used to define these levels (Goal, Purpose, Outcomes, and Inputs) may seem arbitrary, the concept each term expresses is not. The level at which Objectives sit in the project's causal hierarchy has particular and precise meaning. The specific word is not important, but the meaning attached to that word is crucial. If you wish, substitute your own terms.

Think of these various Objectives as rungs on a ladder. The logic which links these levels permits a disciplined approach to project design. By getting it out of people's heads and onto paper, you can *test* the soundness of any approach and fill in the missing gaps required to deliver high level impact.

In general, project teams ***manage*** Inputs which ***produce*** Outcomes to ***achieve*** a Purpose which ***contributes*** to Goals. Inputs and Outcomes are generally within the control of the project team, while Purpose and Goal are beyond direct control. However, Purpose is the essential aiming point, and the best measure of project success.

Here are more examples:

Strategic Hypotheses - Business Examples

Objective	Weapons Systems	Disaster Recovery	Customer Service
Goal:	Military capability enhanced	Ensure company can operate smoothly despite unforeseen disasters	Better customer service
Purpose:	Weapons System deployed and ready to use	Recover quickly from a disaster	Employee use new procedures
Outcomes:	1. Weapons system built & tested	1. Emergency power systems in place 2. Data backed up in real-time	1. New procedures developed 2. Staff trained in procedures
Inputs:	1.1 Design system 1.2 Build system	1.1 Install systems 1.2 Test systems 2.1 Identify critical data 2.2 Backup data in real-time	1.1 Create task force 1.2 Develop procedures 2.1 Create training 2.2 Train staff

Good project design requires that a strategic project hypothesis has only one Goal and one Purpose, but it usually has more than one Outcome. Each Outcome can have multiple Inputs, which are the main tasks needed to get there. In addition, reaching a big Goal may require multiple project thrusts, each in a separate LogFrame with its own Purpose and sharing a common Goal.

Strategic Hypotheses - Personal Examples

Objectives	Career Planning	Improve Quality of Home Life	Become a Golf Pro
Goal:	Make money, have fun & contribute in my career	Enjoy my family & give children safe place to play	Beat Tiger Woods & become #1 in the world
Purpose:	Increase my career mobility & market value	Create the ideal back yard environment	Become a tournament golfer
Outcomes:	1. New skills developed 2. Contact network expanded	1. Landscaping completed 2. New children swing & play ground put in place	1. Improve my putting 2. Improve driving
Inputs:	1.1 Attend seminars 1.2 Read business books 2.1 Be more active in community 2.2 Join Rotary	1.1 Hire contractor 1.2 Complete project 2.1 Design playground 2.2 Build playground	1.1 Get new glasses 1.2 Practice daily 2.1 Buy new clubs 2.2 Take lessons

In these examples, observe how the Goals tend to be global, general, and influenced by many factors other than our project. Understand the important distinction between Outcomes and Purpose. Outcomes are what the project team can deliver or make happen, and teams can be held accountable for these. Purpose is the expected impact from the deliverables. Outcomes are things largely within the team's control, while Purpose and Goal are beyond their direct control.

When your project team understands these distinctions, they can focus on delivering the right set of Outcomes, aimed at an important Purpose and Goal shared by senior management and critical stakeholders.

Key Points Review

1. The essence of smart planning is captured in two words: ***if-then***. *If-then* thinking results in a sound design of strategies, projects, and action initiatives of all types.

2. Every project implicitly centers on a set of linked hypotheses, but these are seldom put out on the table for discussion, review, and improvement. Clearly identifying your underlying hypotheses lets you design projects from a strategic, scientific, and management perspective.

3. Sharpening the strategic hypotheses of your project – the chain of *if-then* connections – leads your team to common understanding and agreement on how the project deliverables ripple up to impact business Goals.

Answers to If-Then Exercises

Example #1:

- Get rich and move to Fiji

  ▲

- Become "the hamster giant"

  ▲

- Breed prize hamsters

  ▲

- Find a mate for Orville
  the hamster

Example # 2:

- Live happily ever after

  ▲

- Find my soul mate

  ▲

- Meet lots of prospects

  ▲

- Join an online dating service

Example #3:

- Have happier employees

  ▲

- Reimburse employees faster

  ▲

- Implement new expense
  reporting system

  ▲

- Design new expense
  reporting system

Example #4:

- Improve corporate productivity

  ▲

- Have staff use standard
  procedures

  ▲

- Develop and publish
  best-practice procedures

  ▲

- Identify ineffective practices

Answers to If-Then Exercises (continued)

Example #5:

- Become a CEO by age 40

  ▲

- Get promoted faster

  ▲

- Get my MBA degree

  ▲

- Take part-time classes

Example #6:

- Become a sought-after
  industry expert

  ▲

- Increase my professional
  reputation

  ▲

- Write and publish articles

  ▲

- Identify needs in my field

Example #7:

- Increase corporate profit

  ▲

- Increase corporate sales

  ▲

- Market product successfully

  ▲

- Develop new product

Example #8:

- Save lives and reclaim land

  ▲

- Deploy device in war-torn
  countries

  ▲

- Develop portable land-mine
  detector

  ▲

- Get research funding

Chapter 3: Introducing the Logical Framework

"Make no little plans: they have no magic to stir men's blood and probably will, themselves, not be realized. Make big plans; aim high in hope and work, remembering that a noble, logical diagram, once recorded, will not die."

– Daniel H. Burnham,
American architect and urban planner (1846-1912)

The Best Solutions Tool You'll Ever Find

Three decades ago I worked with an innovative management consulting firm which developed a systems thinking tool, called the Logical Framework, to help USAID (United States Agency for International Development) more effectively plan, implement, and evaluate the thousands of projects in their multi-billion dollar foreign aid program.

Today, the "LogFrame" is widely-used, primarily in international development agencies. The corporate and technical world, however, is just beginning to discover this thinking approach.

The Logical Framework structure appears as a 4x4 matrix which organizes project information in a specific way, using standard management terminology. Each cell in the matrix is organized by interlocking principles of good management and common sense. As you'll see later, the cells interact with each other and changes in one can affect the others, reflecting the dynamics of our thinking process. The completed matrix can communicate a complicated project clearly and understandably on a single sheet of paper.

At first glance, the LogFrame matrix may seem complicated and intimidating. To make it easier understand and use, I recently developed the *Four Critical Strategic Questions*. These four questions offer a simple and jargon-free way to learn and apply the concepts in the LogFrame grid. These questions are inherently embedded in the LogFrame matrix and answering them helps you design your project in a way that covers all the important issues.

Tackling the Four Critical Strategic Questions

The LogFrame captures, in various cells, the answers to the four Critical Strategic Questions:

1. **What Are We Trying To Accomplish And Why? (Objectives)**

   The first column describes Objectives and the *if-then* logic linking them together. The LogFrame makes important distinctions among various "levels" of objectives: strategic intention (Goal), project impact (Purpose), project deliverables (Outcomes), and the key action steps (Inputs).

2. **How Will We Measure Success? (Measures and Verifications)**

   The second column identifies the Measures of success for Objectives at each level. Here we select appropriate Measures and choose quantity, quality, and time indicators to clarify what each Objective means.

   The third column summarizes how we will verify the status of the Measures at each level. Think of the Verification column as the project's management information and feedback system.

3. **What Other Conditions Must Exist? (Assumptions)**

   The fourth column captures Assumptions; those ever-present, but often neglected risk factors outside of the project, on which project logic depends. Defining and testing Assumptions lets you spot potential problems and deal with them in advance.

4. **How Do We Get There? (Inputs)**

   The bottom row captures the project action plan: who does what, when, and with what resources. Software fits here to flesh out the tasks and action plan details using conventional tools like Work Breakdown Structures (WBS) and Gantt chart schedules.

The experience of my clients demonstrates that the LogFrame facilitates collaborative up-front planning and accelerates the process of developing a sound project strategy. For small and medium size projects, this may be the only planning tool you'll need. For projects of any size, this tool is the ideal starting point to help your team systematically and rapidly design a project that can make a real impact.

The LogFrame Matrix

Objectives	Success Measures	Verification	Assumptions
Goal			
Purpose			
Outcomes			
Inputs			

Definitions of LogFrame Strategic Matrix Elements

Objectives	Success Measures	Verification	Assumptions
Goal ▶ Big Picture Objective to which Project Purpose contributes	Measures of Goal Achievement (quality, quantity, time)	Data sources to monitor and verify Goal	*To reach Goal:* External conditions needed to reach Goal and beyond
Purpose ▶ Change expected from producing Outcomes ▶ Motivation for Project	Success conditions expected at end of Project (quality, quantity, time)	Data sources to monitor and verify Purpose	*To reach Purpose:* External conditions needed to achieve Purpose
Outcomes ▶ Specific Results expected from Project Team ▶ What good managers can "make happen"	Description of completed Outcomes (quality, quantity, time)	Data sources to monitor and verify Outcomes	*To produce Outcomes:* External conditions needed to produce Outcomes
Inputs ▶ Activities, Resources and Responsibilities needed to produce Outcomes	Resource Budget and Schedule	Data sources to monitor and verify Inputs	*To obtain & manage Inputs:* External conditions necessary to obtain and manage Inputs

Grab a Front Row Seat

With that quick conceptual appetizer, let's join one of my workshops. Can a two-day executive workshop be considered a project? Sure. Workshops have all the elements of any project, including specific Objectives, defined time frame, limited resources, new cast of players, and uncertainty. As we proceed, you'll discover that the LogFrame is not a form to fill out, but a systematic thinking template that lets you logically design complicated projects by asking, and intelligently answering, the four critical questions.

1. What Are We Trying to Accomplish and Why?

As you wrestle with that question, you may have written scopes of work or strategic plans to guide you. At other times, you start from scratch with a blank sheet of paper.

When I toss out this question at the start of my workshop, common responses are "learn how to manage projects better," or "learn how to meet objectives," or occasionally, "keep my boss from meddling." The common denominator of the various responses is "learning."

Most of the responses address the *what* part of the question, so I challenge them to answer the *why* part. Then I typically get statements like "deliver successful projects" or "improve my projects." So I diagram this *if-then* linkage on a flip-chart pad.

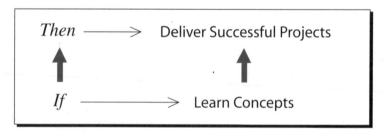

Does this *if-then* logic make sense: If we learn the concepts, then we will deliver successful projects? Sure. This is a logical relationship, but the gap between these two Objectives seems too large, like rungs on a ladder that are spaced too far apart for safe climbing. Learning concepts won't necessarily result in successful projects. I ask my workshop participants, "Is something missing? Would some in-between objective make the linkages more logical? Does something else need to happen between learning and project success?"

After some furrowed brows, they slap their foreheads in an ah-ha moment and exclaim, "Why of course. We need to *apply* the concepts!" Exactly!

Inserting this intermediate Objective makes the *if-then* logic chain more, well, *logical*. Adding this link to the picture, our hypothesis becomes:

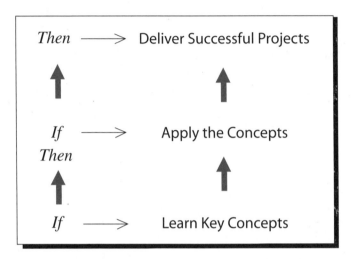

Inserting this extra objective refines our hypotheses and sharpens our focus. Adding "apply the concepts" shifts our focus to that critical, after-workshop Objective that's necessary for successful progress. The need to *apply* becomes the aiming point for designing and delivering learning that can, and will, be put into action.

The Objective "learn key concepts" requires some elaboration to show how the learning will take place. The phrase "conduct the workshop" will suffice for now, and we'll break this out into specific tasks and timing during Question #4.

Logical Thinking By If-Then Linking

Every project consists of multiple Objectives. The Logical Framework tool helps distinguish multiple project Objectives, which exist at different "levels" in the cause-effect chain. The LogFrame organizes Objectives into four separate and distinct levels, defined as follows:

After attaching these definitions, our strategic hypothesis now looks as illustrated on the next page.

Reading from bottom up:

- *If* I conduct the workshop, *then* participants will learn key concepts;

- *If* participants learn key concepts, *then* they will apply them;

- *If* they apply concepts, *then* they'll deliver successful projects.

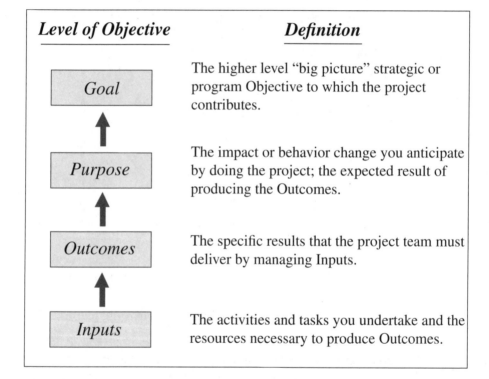

Level of Objective	Definition
Goal	The higher level "big picture" strategic or program Objective to which the project contributes.
Purpose	The impact or behavior change you anticipate by doing the project; the expected result of producing the Outcomes.
Outcomes	The specific results that the project team must deliver by managing Inputs.
Inputs	The activities and tasks you undertake and the resources necessary to produce Outcomes.

We've now constructed a four level, first-cut, strategic hypothesis – the backbone of any project. The logical linkages start with Input activities and percolate up to higher-level Goals. You must climb up each rung in the ladder, step-by-step, without jumping over any rungs.

Note how this strategic hypothesis clearly distinguishes between levels of Objectives: Outcomes (the learning that occurs during the workshop), Purpose (what happens after the "project" – participants *apply* concepts learned) and Goal (the operational benefit expected from the training – better projects). Strictly speaking, Inputs are not Objectives but the tasks and activities necessary to accomplish Objectives.

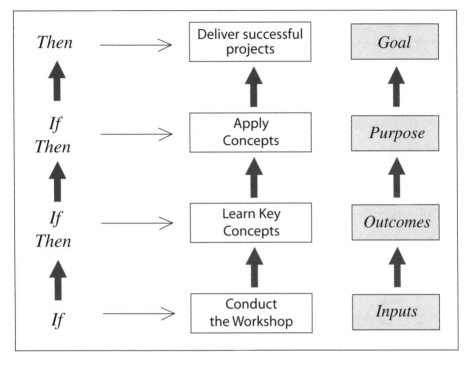

The value of this kind of thinking for your project team should be obvious. *If-then* logic makes it easy to test whether their project hypotheses hang together and connect to business goals. When team members compare and integrate their individual mental models, fuzzy thinking disappears like morning fog evaporating in sunlight.

2. How Will We Measure Success?

Objectives by themselves tend to be ambiguous. Objectives take on shared and mutually understood meaning only when those involved agree how to measure them.

Each level of the LogFrame invites Success Measures which spell out how to recognize the successful accomplishment of each Objective. Success Measures consist of sentences, phrases or bullet points that clarify exactly what each Objective means. They describe, in advance, the conditions that you expect will exist when you declare the Objectives achieved. Together they should spell out Quality, Quantity, and Time – the three most frequent measurements:

- **Quantity** – How many/how much?

- **Quality** – How good? What standards or performance specifications?

- **Time** – By when or for how long?

In addition to these "QQT" categories, two other Success Measurement categories may come into play:

- **Customer** – Who are the customers/clients/users/beneficiaries?

- **Cost** – What resources are required?

Projects also need a feedback and MIS (Management Information System) mechanism to determine whether Measures have been (or are being) achieved. Think of the LogFrame's third column, Verification, as a summary of that system. The Verification column helps you identify the formal and informal sources of data and methods needed to validate the Measures. Typical means of Verification includes physical observations, project team meetings, reports, analyses, tests, and/or whatever else confirms that the Measure has been met.

Let's attach Measures to our example, starting at the Goal and working top down. As we proceed, notice how the interaction among the LogFrame elements enriches our understanding of how to make the project work. LogFrame elements interact horizontally and vertically. Changing the content of one cell impacts others in a logical manner.

Goal Level Measures

I encourage my workshop participants how they will measure the Goal "deliver successful projects." Their responses typically concern, being on-time, within budget, and delivering with quality. An additional Success Measure would be a reduction in problems encountered. All are easily verified through project schedules and financial records. We then insert Goal Measures and Means of Verification into the LogFrame grid shown on page 45.

Purpose Level Measures

Purpose level Measures are the most essential of all because they describe the behavioral changes or conditions we aim for by delivering Outcomes. Purpose Measures describe *project success,* while Outcome Measures only describe *project completion*, an important distinction that is often lost.

I ask workshop participants to detail Success Measures for the Purpose statement "participants apply concepts after workshop." We need to answer, "how many participants," what does "apply" mean, and define "when" and "how well." In small work groups, they come up with possible QQT measures and then merge their answers in consensus.

- Quantity? We decide that at least 80% of participants is a reasonable figure.

- Time? They agree that within six weeks after the workshop is a reasonable timeframe. They also add a second six-month Measure to track the sustainability of the knowledge application over time.

- Quality? Quality, in this case, refers to specific after-workshop behaviors, such as briefing the boss, sharing workshop products, or using the tools on additional projects.

Outcome Level Measures

Outcomes are defined as those deliverables your project team commits to make happen. Think of Outcome Measures as performance specifications, spelling out what the completed deliverables will look like. It's normally easier to visualize Outcome Measures than Purpose Measures because Outcomes are more tangible. For example, the Outcome "participants learn concepts" could have a Measure such as, "by the end of the workshop 90% of participants can apply the four strategic questions and define logical *if-then* hierarchies."

When setting your Outcome targets, keep an eye on your Purpose statement and its associated Measures. Set targets at levels needed to achieve the Purpose-level impact you expect. For example, if the Purpose level quantity indicator was that only 20% of people apply the concepts, it would not be necessary for 90% to learn them. Changes in the Purpose measures affect the Outcome Measures.

As you'll discover with practice, changes in *any* one box can impact several others in a logical fashion. This dynamic and interactive interplay among LogFrame levels leads to the disciplined thinking that creates superior projects. Give thinking process the attention it deserves up front and you'll dissolve innumerable logjams down the line.

Now our project LogFrame looks like the chart on the following page.

Input Level Measures

Take the time to get consensus and clarity on Outcome Measures, and Input Measures, discussed later, will begin to fall into place.

Now, on to the third question:

3. What Other Conditions Must Exist?

No project is a sure bet, even a seminar. Risk factors always exist, whether or not we recognize them. Most teams don't delve deeply enough into defining and testing their *Assumptions* at the start. Assumptions are those uncertain factors which are necessary to complete the logical linkages, but which may be beyond the direct control of the project team. While we can ignore Assumptions, we cannot ignore the impact of ignoring these Assumptions.

In my workshop, I put people in groups again to surface the key Assumptions which link each pair of Objectives. We start by identifying what Assumptions are necessary to go from the Input activity "conduct the class" to the Outcome "apply the concepts." They typically identify such assumptions as:

1. Participants are motivated to learn.

2. Instructor is competent to teach.

Further discussion enriches these initial Assumptions to become:

1. Participants are motivated, able to learn, and actively participate.

2. Instructor has sufficient experience and knowledge to deal with this group.

Note this iterative thinking process that applies to all parts of the LogFrame. First-stab answers get you going, but as you carve deeper and fine-tune the answers, you'll come up with clearer phrasing that more precisely expresses the intentions of your project.

Objectives	Success Measures	Verification
Goal Deliver successful projects	**Measures of Goal** Within next year: 1. Key project objectives reached on-time, within budget at required performance level 2. Fewer problems due to ineffective planning or road-blocks which could have been anticipated during planning (e.g., killer assumptions)	 1. Schedule & financial records 2. Project logs
Purpose Participants apply what they learned following workshop	**Measures of Purpose** 1. Within 6 weeks after training, 80% of participants have: • completed project designs they began during workshop • shared learning highlights with boss & team • explained selected course concepts to others • prepared a LogFrame for additional projects • scheduled in-house training or Rapid Action Planning (RAP) workshop • adapted selected concepts/ tools to enrich their current approach 2. After six months, all participants' project plans have clear objectives, measures, assumptions; all participants are using team process and involving key stakeholders in design	1. Follow-up evaluation after 6 weeks 2. Evaluation after 6 months
Outcomes Participants learn key concepts & tools during workshop	1.1 At workshop end, >90% of participants can correctly: • identify & apply four key questions • define LogFrame terms, set QQT measures • construct logical *if-then* hierarchies • identify & evaluate assumptions 1.2 All teams develop an acceptable LogFrame for a case study in class within two hours 1.3 LogFrame adds strategic value to participant thinking, all walk away with expanded capacity	1.1 In-class exercises, formal tests 1.2 LogFrame passes checklist 1.3 Ask participants

Examining Assumptions can be intimidating, and in some circles, is discouraged as "negative thinking." Many otherwise mature, intelligent people are content with making cursory analyses of the Assumptions-pool and quickly moving on.

Now let's identify the Outcome to Purpose Assumptions, those factors necessary to go from learning to post-workshop application.

1. Participants have the opportunity to apply concepts in their jobs.

2. Participants' boss and organization environment support and encourage application of concepts.

3. Participants can remember materials well enough to apply them.

To get from Purpose to Goal we must assume conditions like:

1. Concepts are relevant – they work in practice and add high value.

2. Organization and its environment are reasonably stable.

Assumptions Expand the Hypothesis

Since Assumptions shine a bright light on potential pitfalls in our climb up the hierarchy, the benefit of identifying them should be apparent, Better to spot these early and decide how to handle them than pay lip-service and have them sabotage us later.

Note that the concept of Assumptions forces us to expand our original hypotheses to reflect uncertainties in our logic chain. The enriched logic becomes *"If/*AND/*Then"* logic.

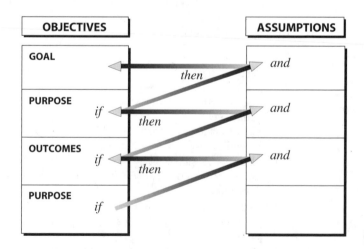

Examine Your Strategic Hypothesis

This leads us to the core idea that distinguishes exceptional project managers from the rest. I call it *The Implementation Equation™*. This equation enriches our thinking by inviting Assumptions to join our *if-then* logic:

The Implementation Equation™:

▷ *if* Inputs plus valid assumptions, *then* Outcomes

▷ *if* Outcomes plus valid Assumptions, *then* Purpose

▷ *if* Purpose plus valid Assumptions, *then* Goal

Every Assumption deserves up-close inspection with a skeptical magnifying glass. The human mind has an infinite capacity to create possible future scenarios with some finite basis in possible realities, but are extremely unlikely, when exposed to the harsh light of critical thinking. Simply stating an Assumption does not make it true. We must ask the following of each one:

- Is this Assumption reasonable? What are the odds it is valid? How do we know?

- What are the consequences for the project if it's not valid? How severe is the impact?

- How can we influence the Assumption in our favor?

Chapter Seven explores how Assumption analysis can point to risks and highlight potential problems. Addressed early, we can adjust the plan to repair some of the weak parts and head off trouble before it starts.

4. How Do We Get There?

With Objectives, Measures, and Assumptions in place, we can confidently turn to the Input level – the action steps to produce Outcomes. Project Inputs are defined as activities, tasks, and resources (time, people, and money). This level is reasonably straightforward and familiar to anyone with project experience. The Input level is where detailed action plans fit, complete with budgets, schedules, milestones, etc. Project management software doesn't help much at the higher levels of Objectives, but works wonders here.

A clear Input task list, detailing the key steps to produce Outcomes, is the basis for implementation. In our workshop example, the Input list consists of the agenda, whose tasks and schedule are carefully tailored to produce the identified target Outcome. Resources include the people in the room, along with training materials (i.e., workbooks, markers, PowerPoint, and of course, coffee).

Ingredients of the Grid

Let's complete this whirlwind tour by looking at all the Logical Framework elements together. If you didn't grasp all the points or nuances, don't worry. The next four chapters will drill deeper into these four questions and associated planning steps. By the end of the book, you'll have seen enough examples to understand and apply the concepts.

Note how cells in this grid connect in an integrated fashion using three directional types of logic, *Vertical Logic* connects Objectives using *if-then* thinking, while *Horizontal Logic* fleshes out Objectives at each level using Measures and Verifications. *Zig-Zag Logic* pulls in Assumptions to ratchet us up the strategic hierarchy, using our now familiar *if-then* thinking.

Objectives	Success Measures	Verification	Assumptions
Goal			*and*
	then		
Purpose *if*	*then*		*and*
Outcomes *if*	*then*		*and*
Inputs *if*			

Strategic Project Thinking Workshop LogFrame

Objectives	Success Measures	Verification	Assumptions
Goal Deliver projects successfully	**Measures of Goal Achievement** Within next year: 1. Key project objectives reached on-time, within budget at required performance level 2. Fewer problems due to ineffective planning or road-blocks which could have been anticipated during planning (e.g.,killer assumptions)	1. Schedule & financial records 2. Project logs	**To Achieve Goal and Beyond** 1. Concepts are relevant- they work in practice and add high value. 2. Organization and its environment reasonably stable
Purpose Participants apply what they learned following workshop	**Measures of Purpose Achievement:** 1. Within 6 weeks after training, 60% of participants have: • completed project designs they began during workshop • shared learning highlights with boss & team • explained selected course concepts to others • prepared a LogFrame for additional projects • scheduled in-house training or project launch workshop • adapted selected concepts/tools to enrich their current approach 2. After six months, all participants' project plans have clear objectives, measures, assumptions; all participants are using team process and involving key stakeholders in design.	1. Follow-up survey 2. Evaluation	**To Achieve Purpose** 1. Participants have opportunity to apply concepts. (Nature of job is suitable) 2. Participants boss and organization environment support & encourage application of concepts 3. Participants can remember materials enough to apply them
Outcome Participants learn key concepts and tools during workshop.	**Measures of Outcomes:** 1.1 At workshop end, >90% of participants can correctly: • identify & apply 4 key questions • identify LogFrame terms, set QQT measures • construct logical If-Then hierarchies • identify & evaluate assumptions 1.2 All teams develop an acceptable LogFrame for a case study in class with two hours. 1.3 LogFrame adds strategic value to participant thinking, all walk away with expanded capacity.	1.1 In-class exercises, formal tests 1.2 LogFrame quality checklist 1.3 Ask participants	**To Produce Outcomes** 1. Participants want to attend, are motivated and open to learning. 2. Needs of group can be met within course design. 3. Amount of time is adequate to cover topics. 4. Instructor is effective with this group.
Inputs **Activities** 1.1 Establish objectives 1.2 Discuss core concepts 1.3 Fundamental Questions 1.4 Preview of the Logical Framework 1.5 Vertical Thinking–Objectives and Hypotheses 1.6 Horizontal Thinking–Measures & Verications 1.7 Identifying and Reducing Risk & Assumptions 1.8 Apply to participant cases	**Schedule** **Day One** 8:30-9:30 a.m. 9:30-10:00 a.m. 10:00-10:45 a.m. 10:45-11:50 p.m. 1:00-2:00 p.m. 2:00-2:50 p.m. 3:00-4:00 p.m. 4:00-5:00 p.m.		**To obtain and manage activities** 1. Workshop facilities adequate to support learning objectives 2. Participants and instructor arrive on time remain present and undistracted during scheduled time.

Answering the Interrogatives

Notice how the structure of the matrix elegantly incorporates answers to the standard "interrogative questions," like *who*, *what*, and *why*. Goal is the big picture program *why*, the rationale for this and related projects supporting the broader strategy. Purpose is the project *why*, the reason for this effort. Outcomes are the *what* that we must produce. Inputs capture the *how*, *who* and *when*.

Real synergy occurs when teams use this tool together. Using the LogFrame builds shared understanding, promotes communication, and increases trust. The LogFrame's common logic and standard vocabulary helps teams get started faster and design strategically-sound projects that deliver.

These tools aren't magic; their power is in forcing you to ask the right questions. Getting the right answers, however, works real magic!

A Rainbow of Applications

You now have been introduced to a potent thought process for designing projects of all types and sizes. Here are some work-related examples of projects that benefit from this approach:

- Preparing a strategic or operational plan for a company, division, or team
- Reorganizing a team and sharpening responsibilities
- Planning how to implement new systems (e.g., MIS, TQM)
- Evaluating an ongoing project to redirect it in a more profitable direction
- Re-engineering a process to improve efficiency
- Defining a logical cluster of projects to support the strategic plan
- Conducting a paper analysis or study (feasibility report, market plan)
- Refining a rough concept into a proposal or action plan
- Analyzing a problem and developing a solution approach
- Planning new products and services from concept through delivery

- Planning research and development
- Implementing initiatives identified through a balanced scorecard

This same thought process applies equally well to non-work and personal projects involving leisure, hobby, fitness, finance, family and "honey-do's" around the house. The list of possibilities is endless, including:

- Organizing church fund-raising events

- Managing a youth soccer team

- Turning your hobby into a part-time online business

- Sharpening plans for professional development, learning and career advancement

- Writing and promoting a book

- Organizing a neighborhood Block Watch program to reduce crime

- Putting together a 25-year high school reunion

- Preparing for retirement

- Raising a loving and supportive family

- Completing an MBA degree part-time

- Remodeling your house

Key Points Review

1. The LogFrame tool provide a common framework, syntax and vocabulary that gives your team a systematic way to:

- Get clear agreement on the big picture

- Establish a joint vision of what success looks like

- Identify the role that Assumptions play in your plan, and how you might influence them

- Spot potential risks and mitigate them in advance

- Define and test the core strategic hypotheses of any project or plan

If A ➡ B, if B ➡ C, if C ➡ D; if D ➡ Bingo!

2. *If-then* thinking is the connective tissue which ties together Inputs, Outcomes, Purpose and Goal. *If-then* reflects a fundamental, *cause-effect relationship* which validates, realizes, and brings practical possibility to your project. It reminds us that *if* we do these things, *then* we'll get this result.

3. We can never totally eliminate risk from our projects or control all the success factors. The best anyone can do is to intelligently manage risk. The LogFrame helps us do this by identifying the Assumptions which are necessary for our strategic logic chain to be valid.

4. Addressing the four critical questions drives the LogFrame process. The matrix elements guide you in answering those questions; the answers fill in the matrix. This interactive thinking tool, step-by-step process, and common language helps your team communicate effectively despite different backgrounds and experience.

You may impress folks with your technical vocabulary, but if you want to speak project success with your fellow team members, you'll want them all using the same vocabulary in the same logical grammatical framework. The four chapters in Part Two will move you forward in learning this new language. As with any other language, to learn it, you must speak it. At first, you may speak haltingly and make mistakes, but by forming those new sounds, saying those new words, and thinking those new thoughts, they will become second-nature.

Part Two:
Mastering the Four Strategic Questions

The LogFrame Matrix

Objectives	Success Measures	Verification	Assumptions
Goal			
Purpose			
Outcomes			
Inputs			

☐ *1. What are we trying to accomplish and why?*

▨ *2. How will we measure success?*

▥ *3. What other conditions must exist?*

☐ *4. How do we get there?*

The LogFrame matrix organizes the answers to these four questions in relationship to each other. Each provides pieces of the project puzzle solution.

The next four chapters go into further detail about these four strategic questions and how they work together as an integrated thinking system.

- Chapter Four explores Question #1 and guides you in defining and aligning project Objectives.
- Chapter Five addresses Question #2 and assists you in pinning down what success means.
- Chapter Six answers Question #3 and leads you through a process to identify and reduce risk.
- Chapter Seven discusses Question #4 and helps you flesh out the work plan.

Chapter 4: Defining and Aligning Objectives

> "Management by objectives works – if you know the objectives.
> Ninety percent of the time you don't."
>
> – *Peter Drucker*

Question #1: What Are We Trying To Accomplish And Why?

Objectives	Success Measures	Verification	Assumptions
Goal			
Purpose			
Outcomes			
Inputs			

Shoot for the Moon

In 1962, President John F. Kennedy committed the United States to landing a man on the moon and returning him safely by the end of the decade. America's grandest achievement was realized in July, 1969, when Apollo 11 completed man's first lunar landing. This was also a grand moment for me, the youngest accredited reporter at Cape Canaveral covering this historic event for a Seattle underground hippie newspaper, *The Helix*. Barely old enough to shave, I sat in the wooden press bleachers among a row of journalists from the world's leading publications, including *Time Magazine, Le Monde, the New York Times*...and *The Helix!*

The evening before launch, the press was escorted to just fifty yards from the majestic Saturn V launch vehicle. Being so near, this 363-foot tall triumph of technology and imagination, bathed in bright Xenon spotlights, made me proud to live in a nation with such a daring vision and go-for-it spirit.

The countdown proceeded through the night and into the next morning until the final seconds... 3 - 2 - 1 Ignition! The massive engines erupted in a fiery plume and the rocket slowly ascended. Even from the press bleachers, two miles away from the launch pad, you could feel the air pulsating from the powerful Saturn first stage engines. I still get goose bumps recalling the thrill of take off as the press cheered with excitement and Dr. Wernher von Braun, watching from mission control, shouted *"Go baby go!"*

Kennedy's bold challenge came during the cold war, the global psychological- political game which the United States seemed to be losing. In 1957, the Soviet Union surprised the world by orbiting Sputnik 1, a three-pound basketball-sized satellite that shocked America into action. Though Kennedy called landing on the moon his *Goal*, his true intention was a higher, unspoken objective. Landing on the moon would demonstrate the superiority of the Western system, and help the United States win the cold war.

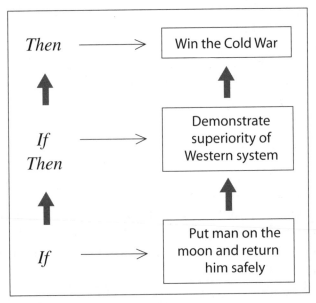

Why is this example significant? Because behind every project rests a higher level motivation of interest to senior leaders. This Objective often gets lost in the hand-off and may not be obvious to those doing the work. If you are a project manager, it's essential to understand the Purpose and the Goal so that you can deliver the Outcomes that will get you there. The LogFrame's Objectives column helps line up project Objectives so they mesh with the broader corporate strategy.

Linking Logical Levels

Whether you aim for the moon or someplace closer to home, making the logical links explicit builds the business case. When you have to convince others and sell your ideas, this is vital. Making the linkages clear is especially valuable in emergent or initiated-from-the-middle projects.

The Logical Framework tool helps distinguish and link multiple project Objectives. The right column in the figure below elaborates on previous LogFrame definitions.

Level of Objective	Definition	Elaboration
Goal	The higher level "big picture" strategic or program Objective to which the project contributes.	• This is the 10,000 foot helicopter view. • Overarching umbrella for multiple projects. • Anchors project to strategic intent.
Purpose	The impact or behavior change we anticipate by doing the project; the expected result of producing the Outcomes.	• Desired change expected after Outcomes produced. • "Linking pin" Objective that's usually missing.
Outcomes	The specific results that the project team must deliver by managing Inputs.	• Deliverables, end products, and processes we can manage. • Team held responsible for delivering Outcomes.
Inputs	The activities and tasks we undertake and the resources necessary to produce Outcomes.	• Implementation plan and schedule. • Project management software helpful here.

Again, our strategic shorthand is:

- "*If* Inputs, *then* Outcomes,

- *If* Outcomes, *then* Purpose,

- *If* Purpose, *then* Goal."

Adding Additional Levels

Can Objectives exist at an even higher level than the Goal? Absolutely. The standard LogFrame illustrates just four levels, but it often makes sense to insert additional levels to more clearly illuminate the *if-then* logic or to tie the project into a high-level corporate objective. Add a higher objective and call it a super-goal, vision, or whatever term you prefer.

A team of scientists from the Los Alamos National Laboratory (LANL) and Sandia National Laboratories (SNL) added a fifth level to their LogFrame to show the cause-effect ripples of their strategy. This Offsite Recovery Project (OSRP) faced the daunting task of organizing a task force of experts to solve a critical national security problem: find a permanent disposal site for some 20,000 "sealed-sources." These were small, neutron-emitting, radioactive sources which had been used by universities and private companies for research, medical diagnostics, and geological exploration.

Many sealed-sources were no longer needed for their original purpose, but there was no convenient process for sealed-source owners to safely dispose of them. Some had been found abandoned in sheds and landfills, posing a serious health, safety, and security hazard. The really scary part was that, in the hands of the wrong people, they could be used to make dirty bombs.

Since these were considered to be civilian rather than military waste, they could not be buried in existing disposal sites due to bureaucratic constraints. Thus, a new site would have to be found somewhere in a state willing to accept them – not an easy task. In addition, no disposal standards existed for this class of device, so these would have to be developed as a part of the project and approved by the Nuclear Regulatory Commission.

The OSRP study team included multiple players from other national research laboratories and from the private sector. Some serious institutional and competitive issues needed to be overcome before productive work could begin. A robust planning approach was crucial, given the wide variety of perspectives among the strong-minded, opinionated players, as well as the technical and political complexity of the problem itself.

In the Objectives column of their LogFrame on the following page, note the highlighted verbs.

The project director chose the Logical Framework tool to get started smoothly. This common language helped them unravel a complex problem

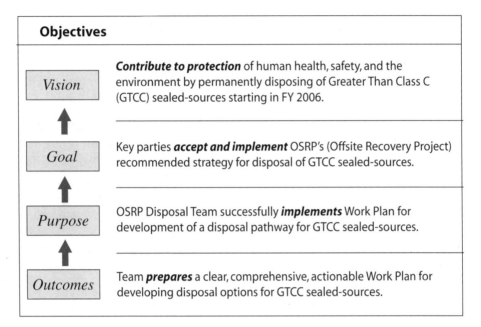

Objectives	
Vision	**Contribute to protection** of human health, safety, and the environment by permanently disposing of Greater Than Class C (GTCC) sealed-sources starting in FY 2006.
Goal	Key parties **accept and implement** OSRP's (Offsite Recovery Project) recommended strategy for disposal of GTCC sealed-sources.
Purpose	OSRP Disposal Team successfully **implements** Work Plan for development of a disposal pathway for GTCC sealed-sources.
Outcomes	Team **prepares** a clear, comprehensive, actionable Work Plan for developing disposal options for GTCC sealed-sources.

into solvable chunks and place attention on some of the critical external factors shaping the success of this Assumptions-driven project. Their initial LogFrame plan served to galvanize the team, point to a common vision, build trust, and develop the task details. (The project's complete LogFrame can be seen at *www.ManagementPro.com.*)

Be assured that the OSRP project implementation is well underway, and by the time you read this, the most dangerous sealed-sources will be off the street and in safe hands. We'll come back to this example in the next chapter and show how the team added Measures to their LogFrame.

Turning a Problem into a Set of Objectives

A problem is simply a project in disguise. Projects masquerading as problems must first be converted into Objectives before you can proceed to solutions. Spend some time carefully diagnosing the problem, because the way you define the problem shapes the range of solution options. Don't get sucked in by an over-simplified definition, catch phrase or symptom. Get at root causes, and find the right problem to solve.

A classic story, first told by systems thinker Russell Ackoff, proves the point that unless you zoom in on the right problem, you risk solving the wrong problem. Tenants in an aging 20-story Chicago office building complained about the long wait for elevators in the lobby. Karen, the owner, was worried that her small business tenants would move to a newer space, so she hired a consulting engineer to solve the slow elevator problem. The elevator was too old for upgrading, so the consultant recommended a new elevator system. The owner gulped at the $300,000 price tag, fearing that she could not increase rents to cover the cost without losing tenants.

Fortunately, Karen got a second opinion from a different consultant. Rather than automatically accepting the problem as "elevators are too slow," this creative consultant suggested that the real problem was that "tenants get bored while waiting." His recommended solution: entertain and distract tenants so they wouldn't mind the long wait. Following his advice, the owner renovated the lobby, installed television monitors tuned to CNN, and mounted mirrors by each elevator so people could preen. Total cost: $3,000.

Solution #1 Objectives	Solution #2 Objectives
Goal: Keep tenants happy	*Goal:* Keep tenants happy
Purpose: Reduce wait time	*Purpose:* Keep tenants from boredom while waiting
Outcomes: New elevator installed	*Outcomes:* Lobby renovated
Inputs: Install elevator @ $300,000	*Inputs:* Install monitor and mirrors @ $3,000

This story illustrates two very different strategies to reach the same Goal, illustrated below in LogFrame language.

Remember this: any problem can be seen differently through the eyes of different stakeholders. To zoom in on the right problem, get alternate points of view. State the problem in different ways, examine its various facets and try inverting each problem statement into an Objective.

Stakeholder collaboration at the front end of the problem analysis stage builds shared understanding, generates more solution approaches, and greases the skids for smoother execution.

Ask your stakeholders:

- What do you see as the problem?

- Why is this a problem?

- How is it a problem, and for whom?
- What causes this problem?
- What are the consequences if we ignore the problem?
- How will you know when the problem is gone?
- What do you think an ideal solution would look like?

Many proven problem analysis methodologies are available, such as the well-known fishbone analysis, the five why questions, basic TQM tools, LEAN Value Stream Mapping, and Six Sigma improvement projects. No matter which methodology you use, it pays to involve your stakeholders early and often in problem identification and analysis.

Terry's Tips for Clear Objectives

Apply these proven tips to make your Objectives stand up straight and salute.

1. Select Just the Right Words

Precise language is a necessary tool for clear Objectives. Perhaps your project Objectives are already described in a work scope or corporate memo. But the quality of the logic behind those can vary tremendously. Some are coherent; others seem to have been written while "under the influence."

Take any given set of Objectives as a starting point only. As you wrap your mind around the situation, you may find that a subtle restatement captures the underlying intent much better. Brainstorm multiple possibilities. Since brainstorming is an imperfect process, your brainstorming list needs to be reviewed and reworked. Before solidifying the language of your Objectives, generate a dozen different answers to Question #1: *What are we trying to accomplish and why?* Experiment with applying different words and sense their nuances. Savor various Objectives, rolling them around in your mind, sensing any sour, bitter, or bland constructs, sharpening and sweetening them for the benefit of all.

Here's the key to well-stated Objectives: state each Objective in a sentence or phrase using carefully chosen *verbs* and *descriptive phrases*. Choosing the just right words is as important as selecting the just right person for a job, so choose well.

On the next page, check out the master menu of Strategic Management verbs you can use to find those just-right, on-the-mark words that best express your true intentions.

As the project starts, Objectives may be fuzzy and ragged, suggesting a general intent or direction but without real clarity. Fuzzy first-cuts are fine. By applying these concepts and iterating, they will become well-formed. Of course, after re-working your Objectives, be sure to validate your interpretation with stakeholders to gain support and ensure you are on target.

2. Unravel Narrative Gobblygook

When I was a program analyst for the U.S. Department of Transportation in Washington D.C., draft Requests for Proposals (RFPs) would sometimes cross my desk. These contained work statements for research studies that would be contracted out to industry and academia. While most made sense, some came across as complex, convoluted, and confusing, with pages of bloated bureaucratic paragraphs that left me scratching my head and worrying about how our tax dollars were being spent.

One day over lunch with the author of an especially suspect RFP, I asked what the real intent was. He confessed that this study would break new ground. The government was not sure what they wanted, but didn't want to come out and admit it. He hoped that by putting enough good-sounding gobblygook in the RFP, some smart consultant would figure out what was needed!

Master Menu of Strategic Management Verbs

- Accelerate
- Accomplish
- Achieve
- Activate
- Administer
- Amplify
- Analyze
- Apply
- Assemble
- Assess
- Assist
- Attain
- Begin
- Build
- Certify
- Change
- Commercialize
- Complete
- Compute
- Convince
- Conduct
- Consolidate
- Construct
- Convert
- Convince
- Coordinate
- Create
- Decide
- Decrease
- Deduce
- Define
- Deliver
- Demonstrate
- Design
- Destroy
- Detect
- Determine
- Develop
- Diagnose

- Direct
- Discover
- Dispose
- Dissolve
- Document
- Educate
- Elevate
- Eliminate
- Encourage
- Enhance
- Enjoy
- Enlarge
- Enlighten
- Enlist
- Ensure
- Envision
- Erase
- Establish
- Examine
- Explain
- Explore
- Evaluate
- Execute
- Expand
- Fabricate
- Facilitate
- Finalize
- Identify
- Implement
- Improve
- Improvise
- Incorporate
- Increase
- Initiate
- Install
- Institute
- Institutionalize
- Integrate
- Introduce

- Invent
- Investigate
- Lead
- Launch
- Link
- Maintain
- Manage
- Market
- Maximize
- Merge
- Minimize
- Modify
- Obliterate
- Obtain
- Operate
- Optimize
- Organize
- Outline
- Persuade
- Plan
- Predict
- Prepare
- Prevent
- Produce
- Program
- Project
- Promote
- Prove
- Provide
- Publicize
- Qualify
- Quantify
- Recommend
- Reduce
- Reengineer
- Remediate
- Report
- Reorganize
- Research

- Resolve
- Respond
- Reverse
- Review
- Revise
- Revitalize
- Revolutionize
- Roll out
- Satisfy
- Save
- Schedule
- Search
- Select
- Sell
- Simplify
- Slow
- Solve
- Speed up
- Spin off
- Stabilize
- Stop
- Store
- Streamline
- Strengthen
- Submit
- Support
- Survey
- Structure
- Synthesize
- Systematize
- Teach
- Test
- Train
- Transform
- Understand
- Update
- Upgrade
- Utilize
- Validate
- Verify

Later, as a management consultant responding to RFPs, I learned a great technique for uncovering the strategic logic inferred in convoluted narrative language. Try it out if you want to separate the extraneous words in project descriptions from the strategic essence.

Certain linking words provide a clear indication of an *if-then* relationship:

• To	• By
• In order to	• Thus
• So that	• That will
• Through	• That

For example, "develop a new customer order system that reduces errors in order to enhance customer satisfaction" includes three linked Objectives. Can you recognize and express them as *if-then* statements?

The best way to connect the dots among Objectives found in a scope of work is to go through the document with a highlighter, marking all of the Objectives you can find (remember, they begin with verbs). Don't be surprised to discover redundancy, with the same ideas repeated using slightly different words. Then search for the connecting words which indicate *if-then* links. With that done, you can recognize the cause-effect relationships and develop your strategic hypothesis – the Goal, Purpose, and Outcomes in the LogFrame.

The terminology found in your project background documents may not match the LogFrame terms. Your documents may use words like Goal, Objective, Outcomes and results without clear definitions of those terms or distinctions concerning what each means.

Don't be misled by terminology – just because something is labeled *Goal* or *Purpose* or *Outcome* does not make it so.

For example, "the project Goal is to develop a safety training program" is not strictly correct. The goal of such a program would be "fewer accidents" or "increased safety." Developing a training program is an Outcome by definition, because it is something you can make happen.

To avoid confusion, look for Objectives that express the meanings found in the LogFrame definitions, regardless of what they are called.

3. Tweak and Fine-Tune

Objectives and mandates that slide down a chain of command or arrive in a memo too often get treated like commandments carved on stone tablets. But many are not fully thought out in the first place and should not be taken as gospel.

If there is a project charter or a scope of work, use it as a starting point. Recognize that, like the first bid in an auction, its real purpose is to get you into the game. Most of them smell of "preliminary draft" and will usually benefit from going through several iterations to get them squeaky clean. Treat the original problem statement and/or scope of work as molded in soft and malleable clay rather than as cast in concrete.

4. Avoid the "Joe's correct" syndrome

As your project begins, keep an open mind about how to best state each Objective. Avoid "premature cognitive commitment," the all-too-human tendency to lock onto simplistic statements that sound good and stop looking for refinements. I call this the "Joe's correct" syndrome.

"Joe's correct" syndrome is a common occurrence when groups brainstorm about project Objectives. Joe is usually a senior manager or respected informal leader who suggests something to which everyone shouts, "Yes! Joe nailed it. That's right!" Joe's words then become written in stone, even though better language might have emerged with more patience. No one suggests any refinements because of "group think" dynamics. Joe himself may later realize that his first stab was a little off-course, but he hesitates to suggest a change because everyone seems sold on his idea. After receiving all of that praise and hook-line-and-sinker commitment, he doesn't want to admit that his idea needs improvement.

Exploring Distinctions Amongst Levels

To fully appreciate the Logical Framework's power, let's explore each level separately and examine the distinctions among the Objectives.

Goal: The Big Picture Impact

The Goal is the big picture context, the overarching corporate or strategic Objective that your project (and usually other projects) contributes to.

Some Goal examples:

- Delight our customers
- Become the top provider in the market
- Increase corporate profits
- Ensure reliability of the nuclear stock-pile
- Foster a climate of innovation
- Be the global leader in safety education.

These trigger questions can help you get to the primary Goal of a project:

- *What is the higher corporate or strategic Objective to which this project contributes?*
- *Why is the project's impact important?*
- *What should happen after we achieve the Purpose?*
- *What is the big picture reason for doing this project?*

The project Goal is often a given. But worthy projects also begin "bottom-up" as a hunch, vague notion or gleam in the eye of a visionary. In these cases, you begin without a clear strategy, and may have to develop, coax out, or infer the Goal. In corporate situations, it can be smart to plug in a hot button Goal statement that your emerging strategy contributes to.

The LogFrame matrix usually shows four levels, but as the OSRP sealed-source project demonstrated, Objectives higher than the Goal can be included to illustrate a higher level of impact. The higher up the hierarchy we climb, the more long-term, general, and "vision-sounding" these "super Goals" become. Alternatively, to maintain conceptual parallelism, or to dovetail with the language of corporate strategic plans, you can insert a level between Purpose and Goal and call it a sub-Goal. You can slice and dice many ways, as long as the basic underlying structural foundation of *if-then* logic hangs together.

Purpose: The Project Focal Point

Purpose is the vital, often missing focus. Purpose expresses the important result or impact we expect the project to produce. Purpose describes *expected change* in system behavior, whether the system of interest is a team of people, a core process, or a new organization unit. Purpose floats a level above that which we can directly control – the Outcomes. Purpose is a subtle concept, often hard to grasp because we are so conditioned to thinking of activities and Outcomes.

Examples of Purpose statements:

- Customers **use** our system (building or delivering the system are Outcomes).

- Core process **improved** (the improvement designs are the Outcomes).

- System successfully **implemented** (developing the system is an Outcome).

- Staff **operates** machinery safely (training them in safe procedures is the Outcome).

Choosing a Purpose statement is the most critical part of project design. Here are some trigger questions you can ask to help identify the Purpose:

- *Why are we really doing this project?*

- *What would the clients or users like to see happen because of this project?*

- *If this project were a success, how would we know?*

- *What impact are we trying to achieve?*

Make Purpose your primary aiming point. Designing projects from the Purpose perspective helps you determine what set of Outcomes you need to reach that Purpose. When you identify a project Purpose, and then define the Outcomes needed to achieve it, you are hypothesizing: "*If* we can produce these Outcomes, *then* we should achieve this Purpose." In other words, select the set of Outcomes that you believe will cause the Purpose to happen. Structure your project design around the strategic hypothesis that, *If* Outcomes, *then* Purpose.

Don't get tangled up in the terms and stumble over whether a project Objective should be called a Goal or a Purpose or a duck-billed platypus. Just keep the *if-then* linkages logical. Confusion often crops up between Goal and Purpose relationships. To determine which is which, test which direction the *if-then* relationship between them makes most sense.

Purpose Drives Outcomes

Purpose describes the change in behavior of the project users or system. Remember, Purpose hovers a level above our direct ability to deliver or control.

For example, if you are responsible for putting in place a new reporting system, the following logic might apply:

Goal:	Communications improved
Purpose:	Managers *use* new reporting system
Outcomes:	System installed

How confident are you that this single Outcome is enough to achieve this Purpose? Hmm...haven't we all seen systems that are built but never used? It seems that an additional Outcome is necessary. Adding this second Outcome adds confidence in reaching the Purpose, and strengthens the strategic hypothesis.

Goal:	Communications improved
Purpose:	Managers *use* new reporting system
Outcomes:	1. System installed
	2. Users trained

Reviewing the Outcome-to-Purpose link, and testing whether or not we have the right set of Outcomes to achieve the Purpose, invites iterative thinking at its best. Continue this dynamic mental modeling process until you come up with what feels like the right Outcome chunks. Mentally examine the Outcome-to-Purpose link. Ask whether or not you have the necessary and sufficient set of Outcomes to achieve the Purpose. Are others needed? Are they collectively sufficient? Are they all necessary? Are these Outcomes the best choices? What other sets of Outcomes might be better?

Purpose is the glue connecting our deliverable Outcomes to the strategic Goal. Choosing a Purpose statement is the most critical part of project design, and the step most often neglected or rushed over.

There may be cases where multiple Purposes are needed to reach the Goal. If so, develop a separate LogFrame for each. For example, reaching the Goal of increased profit margins may require the twin purposes of reduced costs and increased sales. Each requires its own LogFrame with appropriate Outcomes.

Make sure that each LogFrame contains only one Purpose. That makes it easier to align project Outcomes. Multiple Purposes dilute the project focus and weaken the design.

If you seem to have more than one valid Purpose, first check to see whether or not there is a causal relationship among your various perceived Purpose statements. Perhaps you can summarize the multiple Purposes in a single, more global statement.

Many times, what sounds like different Purposes actually expresses the same things in different words. To discover this, ask how you would measure each one. If the Measures are the same, so are the Objectives. Often you will conclude that statements which initially sound like different Objectives actually say the same thing in different words. One may, in fact, be a Measure of the other.

For example, consider two possible Objectives of a safety program "improve employee safety" and "reduce accidents." Which is better?

In fact, accident reduction is a perfect Measure of employee safety.

The most frequent mistake LogFrame beginners make is to choose a Purpose statement which merely restates or summarizes one or more Outcomes. Purpose is the synergistic *result* of Outcomes, not a re-description or summary of them.

Outcomes: What the Project Will Deliver

Project Outcomes describe what the team can, must, and agrees to make happen to achieve Purpose. Outcomes reflect the specific end results or deliverables expected from implementing a series of activities or tasks. Outcomes can be functioning systems or processes (i.e., recruiting process operating), as well as completed end products (i.e., survey completed) and delivered services (i.e., people trained).

Use these questions to help identify required Outcomes:

- *What are your main project deliverables?*

- *What do we need to make happen in order to achieve the project Purpose?*

- *For what end results can the project team be held accountable?*

- *What processes do we need to put in place to achieve Purpose?*

The set of Outcomes constitutes a "management contract," an agreement and commitment to deliver these Outcomes with appropriate resources. This establishes accountability and defines the project manager's job – to produce Outcomes aimed at achieving purpose.

As a rule of thumb, try to structure your projects to include three to seven Outcomes, more or less.

Here's a tip to formulate Outcomes: describe them as they will exist on the day they are completed, using the past tense form of the verb. For example, use "system developed," not "develop system," or "users trained," not "train users." While your fifth grade English teacher might frown, this makes Outcomes easier to visualize in your mind and distinguishes them from activities.

Remember, Input activities are the action steps to produce Outcomes; Outcomes describe what you have after the activities are completed.

Here are some more examples:

Inputs (Activities)	Outcomes
• Train users	• Users trained
• Improve skills	• Skills improved
• Determine best methods	• Best methods determined
• Build new office	• New office built

Test for Necessity and Sufficiency

The Outcome-to-Purpose logic is the heart of your strategic hypothesis. It describes an integrated strategy for reaching Purpose. Each Outcome is a *necessary* ingredient in the recipe for a successful Purpose. But they are usually not *sufficient*. The other factors, which are also necessary but outside your control, will be expressed as Assumptions.

Sometimes it's not clear just what Outcomes are needed to reach Purpose, so start with the ones you are sure about. As your thinking progresses, some additional Outcomes required should coalesce in your mind as a set of completed results or deliverables that constitute your best-guess hypotheses, given present knowledge. To optimize your ability to choose the right Outcomes, let's first turn to the concept of chunking.

The Art and Science of Chunking

What's wrong with this picture?

Reprinted by permission

In a nutshell, the problem exemplified in this Bizarro cartoon is bad "chunking." Chunking is the art and science of breaking down something BIG (problem, strategy, goal) into smaller, more accessible "chunks" (components, parts, phases, categories and aspects). This picture captures a common strategic design dilemma – the disconnect between how something is organized and what it aims to achieve.

Note that there are both gaps and overlaps in the bin labels in the cartoon. The bin categories are not sufficiently discrete to enable someone to decide what goes in which basket. (Hmm…a blue bumpy toy elephant?) And some things that may need sorting don't fit in any of them (where does a cue ball belong?). Worst of all, the categories don't relate to the higher Objective motivating the project. (Thank you to Dan Pirarro for providing the picture that explains chunking better than my words can.)

Putting the cartoon in LogFrame terms, the set of Outcomes (items oddly sorted in bins) won't reach the Purpose (users sort recycleable commodities). A better choice of bin categories would be glass, paper, and plastics. In less obvious ways, we build unintended flaws into our project by not being deliberate about our chunking. The logic we use to chunk and organize determines how well we can achieve Objectives. The importance of getting it right deserves examining various possible chunking options, and choosing which one works best at this time.

Keep this cartoon in mind as you chunk and choose the set of Outcomes needed to reach your project Purpose. In addition, be aware of other projects (besides yours) that may also be needed to get to the goal. Thoughtful chunking is also necessary in breaking out the Input tasks necessary to produce an Outcome.

Chunking also comes into play when you define the cluster of LogFrames that constitute a larger program or corporate strategy. Chunking issues are crucial in organizing a project over time and your chunking logic will likely change in subsequent project phases.

Key Points Review

1. It's better to partially succeed in solving the right problem than to fully succeed in solving the wrong one. Sharpen the problem before rushing to solution.

2. While vague, fuzzy Objectives can provide cover – they do not provide focus. Establish clear Objectives with careful use of language. State your Objectives in a phrase using well-chosen *verbs* and *descriptive phrases*. Remember: separate Objectives for Goal, Purpose, and Outcome levels.

3. Keep in mind the important distinction between Outcome and Purpose. Outcomes are what the project team can deliver or make happen. Purpose is the synergistic impact expected from the set of Outcomes deliverables.

4. Time spent examining and challenging presumed *if-then* linkages is well-invested to avoid wishful thinking, ideology, ignorance or baloney masquerading as logic.

5. Do not hesitate to go back up the chain of command with a suggestion for doing something a little different from what was asked for. The person who originated the requirement may not have thought through his or her needs, or the requirement may have become garbled as it was passed down through several echelons of management. You may have a better understanding than the requester of what he or she needs, should have, or what is possible to do.

Application Step #1

For best results, invite a few core team members to gather around a white board to define and align Objectives. You can also do this on your own, following these steps.

1. Create a draft list of Objectives. Take from a work scope, if one exists; otherwise brainstorm.

2. Group your Objectives into those you can make happen and those you cannot. The former will become Inputs and Outcomes, while the latter will be Purpose and Goal level Objectives. But they are all still in the draft.

3. Review for logical *if-then* relations among them. Discard redundant statements and incomplete thoughts.

4. Tentatively select the highest objective and make it the Goal. Identify one or two Outcomes that will be necessary. Then fill in a connecting Purpose statement. When adding Measures (our next step), you will find insights to refine them until they feel right.

5. Test the logic of your Strategic Hypothesis (Outcome to Purpose to Goal Linkages). Make sure this project backbone is strong. Be willing to iterate and improve the wording.

Chapter 5: Setting the Bar for Success

"What's easy to measure isn't always important;
what's important isn't always easy to Measure."

– Albert Einstein

Question #2: How Do We Measure Success?

Objectives	Success Measures	Verification	Assumptions
Goal			
Purpose			
Outcomes			
Inputs			

Winning the Peace After Winning the War

My appreciation of the Logical Framework's power to tackle the big hairy audacious goals multiplied after I served as a consultant to His Excellency the Wali of Dhofar, in the Southern Region in the Sultanate of Oman. Oman is a small Arab country tucked beneath Saudi Arabia on the edge of the Arabian Sea. While this example may seem far from your field of work, it shows how the LogFrame can organize people to plan and execute an ambitious and complex change strategy.

In the mid 1970s, Oman was wracked by Chinese-backed insurgents from Yemen who enticed some of the local unemployed population to rebel against the government. Following years of fighting, the war ended after the government finally found a compelling way to convince the rebels to lay down their arms and surrender: they paid them in cash.

Having won the war, His Excellency then shifted his attention to "winning the peace," a much tougher proposition. At the time, Oman's population consisted primarily of nomadic herdsmen without permanent homes. The herdsmen had to constantly move their cattle in search of scarce water, whose location varied with shifting rainfall patterns.

The government's strategy was to put in place a community infrastructure which would encourage stable villages to become established. His Excellency believed that by drilling deep wells and creating several dozen year-round water sources, herdsmen would settle down in permanent locations.

In each community, the government would also put in place Outcomes such as schools, health clinics, mosques, and markets. This new physical and institutional infrastructure would, when accepted and used, produce a stable environment for social, economic, and political advancement. In brief, the logic was this:

Goal: Stable environment for social, economic and political advancement.

Purpose: People accept and use infrastructure, settle down permanently.

Outcomes: Institutional infrastructure built (wells, schools, mosques, etc.) in permanent village locations.

This approach had never been tried before and there was no guarantee of success. But without the ability to track progress using well-chosen Measures, the government wouldn't know if the strategy was working, or if the insurgency was in danger of erupting again.

Over a six-week period, I guided government staff from various departments in creating a master Logical Framework, which was exquisitely hand drawn by Indian draftsmen on a six-foot tall vellum document, both in English and Arabic. Between our project working sessions, staff would gather baseline data, consult with local officials, and make field trips to target villages.

His Excellency joined us during the final session, and the team briefed him about the win-the-peace strategy using the LogFrame. The three-hour discussion which followed demonstrated the ability of this tool to target communication around meaningful issues. His Excellency accepted responsibility for influencing certain Assumptions beyond the team's control.

The good news: The program was successful, and today, Oman remains a progressive and moderate Arab nation.

We'll return to the Oman story later, after making some important points about Measures.

Four Features of Manageable Measures

Measures are the instrumentation on your project dash board; choose those needed to intelligently guide your project journey. Don't fall into the trap of measuring only what's easy to measure. Measuring Inputs and Outcomes is most straight forward, but progress towards Purpose and Goal is what really counts. The best Measures meet these criteria:

- Valid – They accurately measure the Objective.

- Verifiable – Clear, non-subjective evidence exists or can be obtained.

- Targeted – Quality, quantity and time targets are pinned down.

- Independent – Each level in the hierarchy has separate Measures.

1. Choose Valid Measures

Valid Measures capture the essence of an Objective, such that changes in the status of Measures accurately reflects changes in the status of the Objective. Let's assume that you manage an internal corporate service function such as Personnel or Finance. Given the Purpose in the LogFrame below, which four of these nine Measures seem most valid?

Objectives	Success Measures	Verification
Purpose An effective and responsive organizational unit	1. Fully staffed 2. Achieves objectives in annual plan 3. Comfortable and efficient facilities 4. Operates within budget 5. People arrive at work on time 6. Meets customer expectations 7. High morale 8. Provides results within "x" days of request 9. Admired by the boss	

The even numbered Measures are most valid. We can reasonably conclude that an organization that achieves its Objectives, operates within budget, meets customer expectations, and provides results within "x" days is indeed effective and responsive. None of the odd numbered Measures pass the validity test.

Admittedly, the unit may need to be "fully staffed" and have "comfortable facilities" (Measures #1 and #3). However, you cannot observe that it's fully staffed with comfortable and efficient facilities and conclude that it is effective. Note this subtle distinction: being fully staffed and having the right facilities may be *necessary* to be effective, but they are not a Measure of effectiveness. As such, these would be Outcomes, not Purpose Measures.

"Arriving at work on time" (#5) may be vital in some contexts (i.e., aircraft crews, pro ballplayers, or bank officers who unlock vaults), but it is less vital in creative or professional work. Google employees, for example, have freedom to show up when they choose.

Another distinction: "high morale" (#7), may be present in an effective unit, but its presence does not prove a state of effectiveness because high morale can occur for many of reasons (great pay, barrels of fun, friendly folks, and daily donuts, to name a few). There is some correlation, but not causation.

Finally, being "admired by the boss" (#9) never hurts, but some bosses may admire for reasons that do not include effectiveness.

2. Make Your Measures Verifiable

Over a century before the expression GIGO (Garbage In-Garbage Out) entered our vocabulary, the Measurement/Verification problem was summed up as follows:

> The government ministries are very keen on amassing statistics. They collect them, raise them to the nth power, take the cube root, and prepare wonderful diagrams. But you must never forget that every one of these figures comes, in the first place, from the village watchman, who just puts down what he damn well pleases.
>
> – *Sir Josiah Stamp, 1911, English economist (1880-1941)*

The village watchman, and their modern-day equivalents, will be found in the Verification column. This third LogFrame column describes processes and mechanisms for determining the status of Measures in Column Two. Today's versions of village watchmen range from no-tech to low-tech to high-tech.

Here are some examples:

- Staff meetings
- Decision meetings
- Financial reports signed
- Industry financial comparisons documentation
- Direct observation of behavior
- Instrument reading or test results
- Employee/management meetings
- Industry surveys
- Customer surveys
- MIS reports
- Letters of agreement
- Completed

- Evaluation meetings
- Focus groups
- Industry certification
- 360 degree feedback

Measurement demands objective and verifiable evidence, not subjective interpretation. Personal opinion is no substitute for verifiable Measures. Here's Leon Rosenberg's rule of thumb for whether Measures are objectively stated: "If being truthful, both a project skeptic and an advocate would agree on the degree of achievement, based on the data presented."

Choose your measures and verifications carefully. The usefulness of a Measure is determined by how efficiently you can gather accurate data to verify it. A project to train in-home health care nurses initially chose "observe nurses in practice" as a means of Verification, but later realized that it was too expensive and unreliable to send people along to watch nurse performance. The team substituted "record of complaints" as an easy-to-track proxy. Let's add means of Verification to the valid Measures of our earlier example:

Objectives	Success Measures	Verification
Purpose An effective and responsive organizational unit	1. Achieves objective in annual plan 2. Operates within budget 3. Meets customer expectations 4. Provides results within 'x' days	1. Quarterly & annual reviews 2. Monthly budget reports 3. Periodic customer survey 4. Tracking logs

Avoid highly subjective verifiers. For example, if you wanted to measure service quality at your local department store, stopping shoppers leaving the store to complete a survey about service would not give you valid data. Only people with plenty of spare time would stop, so the data would be skewed, only representing a portion of possible opinions.

Think of the Verification column as your project management information and learning system. It forces you to define and concisely summarize how information will be generated, tracked, analyzed, and reported. Look first for already existing and easy-to-use methods, then supplement those as needed. Remember to collect not only data that shows progress, but that which warns when you are off track. Having your project team discuss the most effective means to verify your Measures should stimulate creative thinking about how the team will perform, learn, and evolve over time.

Questions for Choosing Means of Verification

- *What kind of data will be collected? How and how often?*

- *Where specifically will we collect this data, and who will do it?*

- *How will data be turned into usable information?*

- *How will that information be used? By whom?*

- *Who else will it be shared with? By whom?*

- *How will it be analyzed and reported?*

- *Are there more cost-effective means of Verification?*

---

3. Target Your Measures

The process of putting numbers and dates on Measures is called targeting. Begin with the basic indicators, and then elaborate on the required quantity, quality, and time (include cost and customer Measures, if appropriate).

a. Choose the Basic Indicator

Managers use new reporting systems.

b. Add Quantity (how much)

80% of level 1 and 2 managers use new system.

c. Add Quality (what kind of change or how good a change)

90% of users rate new system as better than the old system.

d. Add Time (by when), Cost, and Customer (Who)

80% of level 1 and 2 managers use new system by October 1, and 90% of users rate new system as better than the old system.

How do you determine the right target amounts? Choose targets that are sufficient to achieve impact at the next higher level. Setting target Measures is often accomplished by stakeholders negotiating on what is realistic, do-able, and warranted. As a first step, you might write in the indicators, but leave blanks for the numbers and dates unless they are readily known. Otherwise, just specify the indicators and set targets after further analysis or consultation.

The targeting process can boil down to negotiated agreement, or reliance on past experience. When all else fails, choose a reasonable SWAG (Scientific Wildly Amazing Guess).

Here are some examples of how targeting makes vague Objectives come alive.

Vague	*Better*	*Best*
• Improve Sales	• Improve sales by 30%	• Improve sales of product "X" by 30% in 6 months; with half of increase coming from new customers
• Improve Teamwork	• Reduce team conflicts	• Reduce team conflicts requiring medical care by 40% next month

How many Measures does each Objective need? Choose the minimum number that clearly demonstrates the progress toward, and achievement of, each Objective. While a single Measure will sometimes suffice, multiple Measures are usually necessary for all but the simplest Objectives.

4. Choose Independent Measures at Each Level

Because Goal, Purpose, and Outcomes are separate and independent Objectives which exist at different levels, it makes sense that their Measures must be separate and independent as well. It's logically fallacious to expect Measures at one level to capture performance at another level. Remember that Measures *describe* the Objectives, they do not *cause* them.

Returning to our workshop example in Chapter 3, would you accept "80% of participants *learn* concepts" as a valid Measure of the Purpose objective "Participants *apply* concepts after workshop?" Just say no. Participant learning is an Outcome in this LogFrame, Purpose Measures would have to describe the behaviors that constitute "apply."

Keep in mind that the nature of Measures at each level varies.

Goal Measures tend to be broad macro-Measures that include the long-term impact of one project or of multiple projects aimed at the same Goal.

Purpose Measures describe those conditions we expect will exist when we are willing to call the project a success. Defining Purpose level Measures can be tricky, because Purpose often involves expected change in the behavior of people or a system as a result of delivering project Outcomes.

Outcome Measures describe specific tangible results that the project team can and commits to make happen. Describing them as completed results (the "ed" verb form, such as "system developed" or "training completed") makes them easier to visualize in your mind's eye.

Input Measures deal with activity, budget, and schedule. They are described further in Chapter Seven.

Remember what Measures are designed to do: create a shared understanding of what conditions will exist when the Objectives are accomplished.

Measures Sharpen Vague Objectives

The OSRP sealed-source recovery team mentioned in the last chapter employed the LogFrame to build consensus on strategy and produce their primary deliverable – a comprehensive work plan. Clear Outcome Measures enabled team members to agree on what the work plan would consist of, and what they were shooting for, even before they knew its specific technical content.

Success Measures Clarify Project Objectives

Objectives	*Success Measures*	*Verification*
Outcome:	**End of Project Status:**	
Team prepares a clear, comprehensive, actionable work plan for developing disposal options for sealed-sources.	1. By 4/30, a plan has been completed which specifies a logical process for identifying options, conducting analyses, and selecting the preferred pathway for disposal of sealed-sources.	1. Completed document
	2. The Action Plan identifies key tasks, responsibilities, schedules, assumptions, and budgets to complete the appropriate analyses.	2. Inspection of plan
	3. The Action Plan is based on the Logical Framework or equivalent planning concepts.	3. Peer review of plan
	4. The Action Plan development process includes involvement of key project stakeholders.	4. Attendance records
	5. The Action Plan formally allows for effective task coordination and communication among team members.	5. Team member feedback
	6. The Action Plan budget and schedule supports the DOE baseline planning process.	6. Budget analyst feedback

Make Your Measures Rich and Robust

Like masterfully brewed Kona coffee, the best Measures are rich and robust. They are rich in capturing the essence of the Objective, and robust in providing a way to monitor and manage this project element.

The Oman project Goal was a "stable environment in which social and economic conditions improve throughout the Southern Region."

The complexity and multiple dimensions of this Goal required a comprehensive set of Measures and Verifications, as shown in a nearby figure.

The full LogFrame provides a fascinating look at a strategy to win the peace after the insurgency. You'll find this and others at: *www. ManagementPro.com.*

Choose Good Verifiers

An insightful story from the Oman community development project shows what can happen when you don't have good means of Verification in place. To provide health care in 15 isolated rural areas, the Omani government set up a "flying doctor service," whereby health aides would helicopter to remote areas weekly to provide services.

To stem the possible outbreak of a particular disease, they planned to inoculate 95% of the population in these remote villages in 12 weeks. They estimated the population to be 6,000 and ordered twice the amount of vaccine necessary to provide a buffer against possible spoilage. Their means of Verification was to count the number of inoculations given. Great verifier, right?

Objectives	Measures	Verification
Outcomes		
1. Population inoculated against disease.	1. 95 % of population of 6,000 people inoculated within 12 weeks of project start	1. Count inoculations given

Logical Framework for
Winning the Peace After Winning the War

This detailed LogFrame example shows long-term strategies for establishing peace through community development in the Sultanate of Oman, a pro-western ally adjacent to Saudi Arabia.

OBJECTIVES Logical hierarchy of if-then objectives.	MEASURES Conditions which indicate that objective have been achieved.	HOW TO VERIFY Source of evidence to verify measures	ASSUMPTIONS Additional factors necessary for success
GOAL: Stable environment in which social and economic conditions improve throughout Southern Region/Dhofar.	**1. Literacy rate improves:** a. Percentage of persons who can read and write at 3rd grade level increases from ___ % in 1977 to ___ % in 1982. **2. Health standards improve:** a. Percentage of population affected by diarrhea, tuberculosis, trachoma, and other high-incidence illnesses and diseases declines from ___ % in 1977 to ___ % in 1982. **3. Security situation improves:** a. Percentage of population carrying weapons declines from ___ % in 1977 to ___ % in 1982. b. Military incidents and injuries or death resulting from armed conflict declines from ___ % in 1977 to ___ % in 1982. c. Number of enemy "adoo" who have not surrendered declines from 1977 estimate of ___ to a number which is effectively nil by 1982. **4. Economic well-being improves:** a. Average per capita income from productive work activities reaches ___ by 1982. b. Income distributed such that percentage of population at or below "marginal" level as defined by government is less than ___ % in 1982. c. ___ persons employed in livestock, agriculture and fisheries by 1982. ___ persons employed in ___ enterprises which are non-agriculture or fishing by 1982.	1. Ministry of Education figures and estimates. 2. Ministry of Public Health figures and estimates. 3. Ministry of Defense figures and estimates. 4. OHEW figures and estimates.	Assumptions to reach goal 1. Providing direct improvements in the health, education and economic status of Dhofaris will result in the support of the government, rejection of insurgent influence and national unification and stability. 2. Maintaining population in the Jebel, Negd and coastal areas and preventing mass migration to Salalah is essential. Providing direct services to those areas is a means of encouraging permanent settlements and the development of communities.

On the day that I accompanied the flying doctors, long lines of Omani villagers were already waiting when the choppers arrived. They seemed eager to get their injections and the early results were impressive. After just 4 weeks, project records showed some 4,500 people had received inoculations. In the fifth week this jumped to 5,700; in week six it passed 6,000. The eighth week, even more people showed up, and the figure climbed to 7,500 people.

Wait! Something was wrong. After ten weeks, their records indicated that they had injected 9,000 people, 150% of the estimated population! The people in charge huddled and concluded that their population estimates must have gone haywire. Only later, after interviewing villagers, did they discover the true problem.

Here is what happened. Less than 20% of the population had actually received a shot. But this same 20% kept returning week after week on the false belief that if one injection is good for you, lots of them are even better!

Program management fell into the trap of measuring what's easy to measure (number of inoculations) rather than what was really important (who actually received inoculations). With a more valid way to verify, they would have detected the problem earlier. Chalk it up to inadequate education, poor means of verification, and the lag time in analyzing collected data.

The Power of Purpose

Purpose Measures are the most important in the hierarchy. Why? Because that's your primary aiming point, the what-should-occur result you expect *after* you deliver what you can. Goal is important too, of course, but Goal Measures often reflect the result of multiple projects and outside factors and are, therefore, not impacted by your project alone.

Set Purpose Measures before you set your Outcome Measures. That way you can target and tailor your Outcome Measures at levels sufficient to achieve the Purpose level impact (as indicated by Purpose Measures). The act of defining these establishes the synergy between the Outcomes and Purpose.

From Here to There

Purpose level Measures describe the result of a transformation, from the way things currently are, to how we'd like them to be. Purpose Measures reflect your "walk-away feeling proud indicators;" the conditions that would be in place when you declare the effort a success.

Many projects involve managing "soft" factors such as attitude and behavior shifts. These hard to describe changes can be clarified using "from-to" language. Ren Powers, an accomplished IT project manager, was responsible for an education campaign for employees in a financial service firm whose laptops carried sensitive financial data. Employees sometimes bypassed the recommended security procedures because they seemed cumbersome and took more time. Her project Purpose was that "employees understand the need for security and follow defined procedures."

From (The way it is now)	To (How we want it)
• boring and useless	• interesting and helpful
• outdated and old	• future and cutting edge
• pain in the ass to do	• easy to comply with
• old-fashioned "fuddy duddy"	• innovative
• only benefits me at work	• helps my entire life
• roadblock	• enabler

These insights helped her develop a program designed to shift attitudes before attempting to shift behavior. Outcomes included the roll out of a compelling and entertaining online cartoon featuring a black panther, coupled with "Panthergrams" – monthly newsletters with articles on personal and business security issues. Remember that having a clear sense of Purpose – pinned down with Measures – gives an aiming point for the Outcomes.

She recognized that changing their attitudes about security procedures was the key to behavior change. Her Purpose Measures were stated using a from-to analysis illustrating necessary employee attitude shifts.

Managing Complex Enterprise-Wide Change

There was trouble at the Fircrest School for the Developmentally Disabled, home to some 800 adults and children who suffered from serious physical and emotional developmental disabilities. Fircrest is funded both by Washington State and Federal funds, and managed by the Washington State Department of Social and Health Services.

A few years ago, several disturbing incidents indicated that residents were being improperly treated and their quality of life was low. There were some unexplained injuries to residents and even one suspicious death. Visiting experts noted overuse of psychoactive medications and restraints. Quality assurance was lacking. Medical and nursing care records were not timely and accurate. Too many nurses were assigned to administrative duties and too few to resident care and treatments.

Following an audit, the school's federal certification was revoked, along with millions of dollars of federal funding. This presented management with a serious problem that needed solving quickly and effectively. Project Manager Katie Cameron used the Logical Framework with her project team to develop a strategy to improve the safety, health, and quality of care in order to regain federal certification.

Their Purpose statement appears on the next page, rich with excellent Measures and Verifications. Note how the Measures pin down what would otherwise be a vague Purpose. There are enough specific and targeted Measures, along with related data sources, to permit an evaluation of the project's impact.

Notice the interplay among the horizontal elements of Objectives, Measures, and Verifications at each level of the LogFrame. This "horizontal thinking" builds a common vision based on Objectives that can be measured and verified. The full Fircrest LogFrame is included in the Appendix to demonstrate best practices usage. You'll note that it is jargon free and easy to follow.

The good news: the Fircrest project team successfully implemented their action plan and regained certification. Today, they are one of only three such schools in the nation that continue to meet federal standards.

Measuring the Purpose of an Enterprise-Wide Change Project

Objectives	Success Measures	Verification
Purpose: People who live at Fircrest are safe and healthy, receive quality care, and their human rights are protected.	**End of Project Status:** 1. A 50% reduction in resident injuries that require nursing or medical care, or other intervention, occurs between 1/1 and 10/31.	1.1 Review & summarize incident reports. 1.2 Review/tabulate injuries from medical notes
	2. No unusual or suspicious resident deaths occur between 1/1 and 10/31.	2. Review coroner reports
	3. An 80% reduction in restraints and time out use will be achieved between 1/1 and 10/31.	3. Review and summarize restraint & time out records.
	4. A 25% reduction in number of residents being prescribed psychoactive medication occurs between 1/1 and 10/31.	4. Review pharmacy/drug administration records.
	5. 75% of residents are engaged in paid work activities for three more hours per day by 9/1.	5. Collect, review and summarize resident production records & paycheck information.

Special Situations Demand Special Measures

When confronted with stubborn Objectives that are just too difficult to measure directly, consider these three special types of Measures/indicators:

Leading Measures

Look for leading indicators when the key Success Measures won't be available for a long time and you need earlier data to adjust your plan. Leading indicators show up in every context. The index of leading economic indicators accurately predicts economic activity months later. Interest rate changes predict new housing starts. Retail computer sales indicate future microprocessor demands.

The "Big Mac Index" is a leading indicator which has been fun and informal, yet functional, for nearly two decades. According to the theory behind this index, when a McDonald's Big Mac burger is cheaper in a given country than it is in the U.S. (expressed in U.S. dollars), then that country's currency may be considered undervalued, and usually goes up in a short time to correct the imbalance. Don't knock it; as a leading indicator it has made millions for currency traders hip to its value.

The Strategic Project Management workshop LogFrame in Chapter Three included two Purpose level Measures for "participants apply concepts after workshop". But these could not be reliably measured until weeks after the workshop was over, too late for fine-tune adjustments. How could I, the instructor, know during the workshop, whether application was likely or not? The solution was to add this leading Measure, which could be determined during the class.

Objectives	Measures	Verify
Participants apply concepts after workshop	During workshop, 90% of participants identify at least one way to apply concepts and commit to doing so.	Each person verbally shares their plan

With this Measure in mind, I can occasionally ask "tell me how you plan to apply these ideas," and then count the bright faces and eagerly-raised hands, subtract the quiet-faced hand-hiders, and make a good prediction about future participant application.

More important, this leading indicator gave us ample opportunity to modify the workshop pace or emphasis if people weren't getting it. Keeping track at this level (Purpose) versus simply tracking the agenda to maintain schedule (Input level) permitted continually refining the workshop direction to best achieve learning Outcomes.

How nimble is your project? Do you have early warning indicators so you can spot trouble before it strikes! Are you Purpose focused?

Projects which benefit most from leading Measures are those emergent or "learning by doing" efforts that involve frequent adjustments and ongoing modification in order to redirect the Outcome strategy during implementation.

Proxy Measures

When direct Measures are too difficult, expensive, or unreliable, choose a proxy Measure. Proxy Measures are substitutes that closely correlate with Measures of interest. While proxies are never as accurate as direct Measures, they are often the best you can do.

As a young man applying for a summer cowhand job on a Texas cattle ranch, John Huchton encountered a proxy Measure of his qualifications. To start the interview, the wise and grizzled old ranch boss said, "Show me your pocket knife." The boss carefully ran his thumb across John's knife blade and concluded "It's sharp. You're hired." The boss later explained that a dull blade means a lazy cowboy – one unprepared to quickly cut a rope tangled around a calf's leg, or slice the head off a striking rattlesnake.

What proxies might you use for hard-to-measure process dimensions of your project (as distinct from tasks and timeline)? How will you know that people are engaged and commited? How would you measure open communication. Effective coordination? Stakeholder support? Remember, you can't manage what you can't measure.

Unobtrusive Measures

The very act of measurement can distort data accuracy. The over-bearing boss who asks his timid secretary how she likes working for him will get the answer he wants, not the truth. Unobtrusive Measures come in handy when attempts to measure more directly would produce unreliable results.

Southwest Airlines is famous for friendly flight crews. But it's tough to measure a friendly personality during an interview because anyone can fake being nice for an hour or two. So, in the early days, Southwest went unobtrusive. They would fill conference rooms with groups of prospective employees and ask each candidate to make a brief presentation to the group.

As each candidate spoke, Southwest staff, hidden behind one-way mirrors, watched the facial reactions of the candidates listening to presentations. Candidates were judged not on their presentation delivery, but on how they encouraged and supported the other presenters. Audience members who actively listened and gave encouraging facial feedback were perceived to be just the kind of genuinely friendly folks Southwest wanted distributing their peanut lunches.

One Measure on the Oman LogFrame concerned how secure villagers felt. How could they determine this? The chosen proxy Measure was the percentage of the population who carried visible weapons to the village market.

The Magic of Measures

Adding real-world Verifications and Measures is the crucial step that tethers the grandest of dream Goals to the anchors of reality. Tacking metrics in place not only helps to shake out the dreamy-eyed fluff from a project, but it virtually catalyzes the project's execution by increasing confidence in all who read, study, or hear of the project – precisely because those Measures and Verifications have been consciously and formally embedded from the start.

Setting Measures in advance for Goal, Purpose, and Outcome Objectives is essential. If direct Measures don't work, try proxy, unobtrusive, or leading Measures. Remember that if you cannot measure your Objective with some ease and validity, then you *don't have* an Objective, you have wishful thinking.

Key Points Review

1. Having valid and reliable Measures for all Objectives clarifies them, strengthens confidence in the project design, and reduces later squabbles.

2. Avoid the trap of measuring what's easy, rather than what's important. Inputs and Outcomes are most easily measured, but progress towards Purpose and Goal is what really counts.

3. Make sure your Measures:

- Are specific in terms of quantity, quality, time, customer, and cost.

- Measure what is important about each objective.

- Consist of separate and distinct Measures at each level.

- Pass the validity test – changes in the status of Measures are attributable to changes in the status of the Objective.

- Include practical means of Verification.

4. Objectives that are too tough or expensive to measure demand that you creatively turn to three special types of indicators/Measures:

- Leading indicators give you early feedback about strategy. Use leading indicators when the Key Success Measures won't be available for a long time, and earlier data will help you adjust your plan.

- Proxy Measures are substitutes for direct Measures that correlate with the Measure of interest. When direct Measures are too difficult, expensive, unreliable, or otherwise impossible, choose a proxy.

- Unobtrusive Measures must suffice when attempts to measure the Objective would result in distorted or unreliable data.

Application Step #2

Review the list of Objectives you completed in Step #2 in the previous chapter. Make sure you have a good statement of Goal, Purpose, and Outcomes.

1. Beginning with Purpose, develop clear Measures using QQT (quality, quantity, and time). Use complete sentences, phrases, or bullet points to describe them. Add means of Verification. At the same time you set Measures, decide how to verify them. Measures which can't be verified are worthless.

2. Develop Measures for Goal, along with means of Verification.

3. Develop Measures for each project Outcome, along with means of Verification.

4. Set them aside for a few days and take a fresh look later. Invite input from others. Iterate and improve your Measures; don't freeze them.

In addition, select a few Measures which track the performance of your project team and management process. These process gears need to turn easily and mesh smoothly to deliver project results, and making them measurable makes them more manageable.

Chapter 6: Prevent Problems Before They Strike

"Begin challenging your own Assumptions.
Your Assumptions are your windows on the world.
Scrub them off every once in awhile, or the light won't come in."
– Alan Alda

Question #3: What Other Conditions Must Exist?

Objectives	Success Measures	Verification	**Assumptions**
Goal			
Purpose			
Outcomes			
Inputs			

The Whoops Hall of Shame

When Mars, the maker of M&M candies, was approached by Steven Spielberg's marketing crew, they could not believe that a movie featuring an alien dropping their candies would be a helpful marketing move. So when "ET-The Extra-Terrestrial" was released, it was Reese's Pieces that became an overnight mega-selling candy, much to M&M's chagrin. Whoops!

When a well-known American electronics company first laid out a football-field sized array of television equipment in their Silicon Valley plant, intended to later be moved to broadcast the Summer Olympics in Australia, they missed something: not all countries use the NTSC broadcast format which is standard in America. Asia and Europe wanted to watch the summer games too, but somehow, they forget about the PAL broadcast format used in much of the world. Whoops!

When NASA's $150 million Orbiter crashed into Mars, analysis showed that the spacecraft builders worked in the metric system. However, NASA *assumed*, but failed to *verify*, that the builders were using the English measurement system of feet and inches. Thus, the Orbiter's computer contained bogus data and the mission didn't have a chance. Whoops!

In all of these, and in countless other projects, painful "whoops" consequences sprung from undefined, unexamined, or invalid Assumptions.

Think of Assumptions as the external conditions which must exist for our project logic to be valid. They are conditions over which the project team lacks direct control, or chooses not to exert control.

Faulty Assumptions act as invisible beds of quicksand, waiting to suck good projects under. To be certain, nothing is a sure bet because the world is full of risks that bedevil all human endeavors. While we can never completely eliminate risks, we can reduce them to acceptable levels and prevent nasty surprises down the line.

Assumptions Carry Consequences

Assumptions are often *the* most critical factor in determining how a project turns out. Every project rests on Assumptions, whether or not they are acknowledged or verified. More projects than you might expect fail due to unrealistic and unwarranted Assumptions. Unfortunately, project leaders don't always bother to identify, examine, and validate what they implicitly assume. Every human being naturally makes Assumptions – that's part of the thinking process – but we seldom spotlight them for analysis.

The LogFrame matrix is designed to tease out Assumptions and help articulate the underlying issues and conditions, so you can either deal with them before they become pitfalls, or monitor them and have a "Plan B" waiting in the wings. By flagging troubling Assumptions, you can structure project conversations around risk factors.

Once Assumptions are identified, you can deal with them using methods in this chapter, as well as conventional risk assessment and reduction tools. Handling uncertain Assumptions strengthens confidence in the project hypothesis and helps you sleep at night.

Note that Assumptions outside your sphere of control may be within someone else's control. Sometimes you can coax someone else to make those factors *their* Objectives. After all, there's no limit to what you can accomplish if you can get someone else to do the work.

The sealed-source recovery project was Assumptions driven; several major and uncertain Assumptions show up in their initial LogFrame (see *www.ManagementPro.com)*. Among the major ones, project leadership assumed that they would find a state interested in being a sealed-source storage site. They assumed that key decision-makers had the political will to find a permanent solution, rather than defer the problem to future generations. So, in addition to creating a work plan and doing the technical analysis of possible disposal sites, the project leader "worked the Assumptions column" in an ongoing effort to influence and turn uncertain Assumptions into reality.

Spotting Trouble Before It Comes

How do you spot the most relevant project risks and incorporate them into your LogFrame as Assumptions?

You can start by conducting an environmental scan of what's going on around you, choosing from two levels of scanning. One level of scanning is broad-brush macro; the other is project-focused micro.

Broad-brush macro scans of the larger environment focus on the big picture trends, drivers, and change factors that may impact your plans. This wide-angle scan uses your team's experience to identify the SKEPTIC factors (Societal, K(C)ompetitive, Economic/Environmental, Political, Technological, Industrial and Consumer/Client) and any changes on the radar which may impact your project during its life. (More about this in the free article, "Environmental Scanning," at www. ManagementPro.com.)

This broad brush scan is optional for individual projects, and is more often done during a larger strategic planning process than on a project basis. But doing a localized scan of your more immediate project environment is not optional. Localized scanning is the smartest way to identify which pesky Assumptions to keep an eye on. Ask yourself, "What must we Assume?" or "What *are* we Assuming?" in each of these categories:

- Project Team Members
- Stakeholders Interests
- Management Support
- Technical Issues
- Resource Availability
- Community Factors
- Necessary Skill Sets
- Customer Expectations
- Political Climate
- Competing Issues

If you were assuming that "Bob will be available to give half his time to this project in June," you better check with Bob. He did mention something about taking a long summer vacation in Yellowstone Park.

How the LogFrame Accommodates Assumptions

Think of the Assumptions column as a semi-permeable membrane through which the effects of external factors cross the boundary into your project domain. Recall from Chapter Three how Assumptions force us to expand the original hypothesis to reflect the more important issues in our logic chain. The original *if-then* logic now becomes *if-AND-then* logic, the essential connecting threads which weave together your strategic hypotheses.

Murphy and his infamous law dwell in the Assumptions column. Carefully defining and testing LogFrame Assumptions at each level forces us to consider what is needed to make the project work and design it accordingly. Remember that the intent of working through Assumptions is to spot potential weaknesses in advance, especially the dreaded "killer" Assumptions.

Three Steps for Managing Assumptions

Turn external uncertainty into acceptable risk with this simple, but insightful, three-step process.

1. Identify Key Assumptions

Get your core team together, or fly solo, and use these kick-off questions to surface underlying Assumptions.

- What conditions must exist, and what factors must be true, for our *if-then* logic to be valid?
- How must the world cooperate with us?
- What *else* must happen for this to succeed?
- What else *should* we Assume?

The Museum of Silly-Ass-umptions

The world is full of implicit, unexamined Assumptions where Murphy's Law thrives, such as:

- Once we have management support, we will always have it.
- The people we want on this project will be highly motivated.
- Everyone is in the loop and on-board.
- We already know what our customers want.
- The IRS won't audit me two years in a row.
- I don't need to back up my laptop regularly; it's a brand-name machine.
- One more drink won't hurt.
- This approach will work because it's always worked before.
- This product is so fabulous it will fly off the shelf.
- We all know the project Objectives, no need to write them down.
- Europe's economies are tanking, but that won't affect us.
- We're the only company with this great idea; no one else will think of this.
- With online start ups, profits aren't important, just eyeballs.
- We all share the same goal.
- All stakeholders will participate fully and support the plan.
- Surely they understand how important this is to the organization.
- If we get behind, we can always add more resources and catch up.
- We don't need to examine Assumptions, nothing can go wrong.
- We've anticipated and identified all the important Assumptions.

Brainstorm all the conditions believe are necessary to go from one LogFrame level to the next. Because different Assumptions operate at each level, do this for each linked level (e.g., Input to Outcome, Outcome to Purpose, and Purpose to Goal). An additional Assumptions block appears in the lower right hand box of your LogFrame matrix: Assumptions for and about Inputs. Think of these project pre-conditions, such as "project will be approved and funded," as the initial ante to get the project moving.

Express each Assumption as a positive condition that must exist for your *if-then* logic to hang together. Make them specific, not general. Fuzzy and general Assumptions mask the specific concern behind the Assumption. Turn fuzzy Assumptions into well-defined ones by including QQT Measures. The examples below show the differences between vague and solid Assumptions:

Vague Assumptions	Better Stated Assumptions	Best Stated Assumptions
• Management will support the project	• The VP's of Finance and Marketing will support the project	• The VP's of Finance and Marketing will each allocate $100,000 from their budgets by June 30
• Sufficient resources available	• System analysts are available to help the project	• 6 person weeks of qualified senior systems analysts in June
• Management turnaround time acceptable	• Prompt turnaround on deliverables submitted for approval	• Turnaround on deliverables not more than 5 working days
• Competitive situation stable	• Competitor doesn't introduce similar product in the same time frame.	• Panasonic or Apple doesn't introduce electronic gizmo with similar features at same price point in the next 8 months.

2. Analyze and Test Them

Having defined them, now you can test your Assumptions in order to improve your strategy. Chew on questions like these:

- How *important* is this Assumption to project success or failure?

- How *valid* or probable is this Assumption? What are the odds that it is valid (or not)? Can we express it as a percentage? How do we know?

- If the Assumptions fail, what is the effect on the project? Does a failed Assumption diminish accomplishment? Delay it? Destroy it?

- What could cause this Assumption to *not* be valid?" (this one surfaces specific risk factors).

Addressing these questions will help you decide which Assumptions to include in the LogFrame matrix. Don't list the "sure-thing" high probability Assumptions or the very unlikely and unrealistic ones (i.e., "a wonderful miracle of some sort will happen"). Instead, list those that have a non-trivial probability of being *wrong*, and whose failure could have important consequences for the project. Search for the "deal-breakers" that could seriously harm the project and have a high potential for failure. Root out any unrealistic Assumptions, such as "no turnover of project staff."

Ignore those which are not critical to the causal logic, or which trivialize the design. While it is true that astrophysicists predict that within two decades, an asteroid on a near-earth trajectory has a 1 in 75,000 chance of hitting the earth, the threat is not probable enough to list "no asteroids wipe out our building" among your Assumptions.

Try to assess the degree of risk you can expect from these critical Assumptions by using a simple rating system or probability percentages. This first-cut Assumption analysis can offer a jumping-off point for more rigorous risk assessments, using conventional risk management techniques.

Even when done informally, the Assumptions discussion will surface potential issues for team attention.

3. Act On Them

Now comes the fun part. Put each key Assumption under your mental microscope and consider the following:

- Is this a reasonable risk to take?

- To what extent is it amenable to control? Can we manage it? Influence and nudge it? Only monitor it?

- What are some ways we can influence the Assumption?

- What contingency plans might we put in place just in case the Assumption proves wrong?

- How can we design the project to minimize the impact of, or work around the Assumption?

- Is this Assumption under someone else's control?

- How could we design the project to make this Assumption moot or irrelevant?

Acting on Assumptions requires making contingency plans and putting preventive solutions in place. For example, if it absolutely, positively *must* get there overnight, send identical packages by DHL, UPS and FedEx. If storms are brewing, nail on plywood and get a gasoline powered pump before the hurricane hits. You get the idea.

Once Assumptions have been evaluated, use them to make informed decisions about project design. But making the effort to *identify* Assumptions is the real rub, isn't it? Assumptions are the water in which projects swim, but the fish, it seems, are the last to learn about their watery environment. In other words, people immersed in the daily tasks of doing their job are generally too close to the trees to see the forest. The focus of this part of the Logical Framework is to bring into the realm of *consciousness,* any and all *unconscious* Assumptions which, typically, are most of them.

Making Fine Point Distinctions

Though Assumptions have been defined as factors beyond your control, this is not always true. Let's make some fine-point distinctions about what you can do with Assumptions once they are identified. Here are some options for dealing with them:

- **Monitor and respond** – When the externalities are way outside your zone of control, the best you can do is keep an eye on them. Interest rates, competitor moves, and the cost of commodities are examples.

- **Influence or nudge** – Though beyond your control, you can sometimes influence conditions underlying the Assumption in the right directions. Example: keeping key gatekeepers briefed to maintain ongoing support from senior management.

- **Control** – Often you can, in fact, bring an Assumption into your project as an Objective if you choose to, but this takes more resources. Alternately, you can make sure it's covered as an Objective in someone else's project.

Controlling Assumptions means doing one of the following:

- **Change the Project Design** – Add Outcomes or Input activities to work around the pesky Assumption.

- **Add Tasks** – Create a new project or related effort that will counteract or moot the Assumption.

Finally, you can always choose to:

- **Do Nothing** – Continue "as-is" and accept the consequences. The issues *may* be under your control, but you choose not to worry about them because the risks don't justify the cost, or resources aren't there.

Putting Assumptions to Work

In addition to the distinctions described earlier, Assumptions in the LogFrame grid may perform other functions, including the following:

- **Provide reference point for interface projects.** "System design specifications received from Mike by 3/15." Assumptions which identify interfaces and project interdependencies are a way to link a cluster of projects. Remember that one person's Assumption may be another's Objective.

- **Provide diplomatic conversation starters.** "Senior management support is strong" opens the door to discuss who needs to do what, and when.

- **Incorporate other documentation.** Highlight other documents and analyses. "Findings of the March Market Forecast remain valid."

- **Highlight related projects or LogFrames.** Program strategies are simply clusters of projects supporting the same Goal. The Purpose-to-Goal link should identify all other projects aimed at the same Goal.

- **Compress logical levels.** Objectives stated in the LogFrame's first column may compress complex hypotheses into simpler ones; the Assumptions column provides room to spell out intermediate links. (Our workshop example in Chapter 3 did just that by hypothesizing that if participants apply the concepts, then they'll deliver successful projects. But there is a plausible intermediate link: "*If* participants apply concepts, *then* they'll be better project managers; *if* they're better project managers, *then* they'll have successful projects.")

- **State policy/value judgments.** These show up at Purpose and Goal levels, i.e., "it makes sense for us to enter this particular market."

Boost Your Team's Confidence

Vetting Assumptions as a team enriches your perspective. When finished, you'll have greater confidence in your project design and know what to watch for. By setting up an enterprise-wide radar to scope out incoming and fast-breaking changes, your initiative will be in a strong position to continue to create its "future of choice," even when some ugly change slips in under your corporate radar.

As you and your team become adept at Strategic Project Management, you'll be more certain of your ability to navigate skillfully and courageously across the sea of change washing over all of us.

Key Points Review

1. Assumptions always exist, whether or not we acknowledge or verify them. Many a project failure comes from faulty, ill-formed, undefined or unexamined Assumptions.

2. Assumptions are often the most critical factor in project success. Take time for your team to identify, examine, and validate the Assumptions on which your strategy rests.

3. Look for deal-breaking, project-killing Assumptions early, and make sure they are effectively addressed.

4. Place your Assumptions at the LogFrame level they affect. Assumptions with either very high or low probability should not be in the LogFrame.

5. Make your implicit Assumptions explicit! Get Assumptions out of your head and onto paper.

6. The most useful Assumptions:
   - Are formulated as desirable, positive conditions.
   - Are placed at logical project levels.
   - Include QQT Measures as appropriate.
   - Cover all key outside factors that impact the project.
   - Are backed up by strategies to handle risky and negative impact Assumptions.

Application Step #3

Squeeze out known and knowable bugs and get rid of project risk by examining your Assumptions using this process:

1. **Identify** all key Assumptions in your project, especially the mission-critical (a.k.a. 'killer') ones.

2. **Analyze** their probability and the consequences of their impact, along with the various means and costs of possible deflection or amelioration by your team.

3. **Take action** to manage what you can. Before faulty cause trouble, beef up defenses to prepare for their arrival, and communicate effectively with all stakeholders throughout your project lifecycle.

Review pages 98-102 for the detailed how-to of these three steps.

Chapter 7: Flesh Out the Action Plan

"Planning is bringing the future into the present so that
you can do something about it now"

– Alan Lakein

Question #4: How Do We Get There?

	Objectives	Success Measures	Verification	Assumptions
Goal				
Purpose				
Outcomes				
Inputs				

Getting Traction for Action

In the preceding chapters, you've answered the first three strategic questions and simultaneously fleshed out three major chunks of the LogFrame: *Objectives, Measures,* and *Assumptions.* With those project design elements in place, your attention can now shift to Inputs, the bottom horizontal LogFrame level that deals with rubber-to-the-road action planning. During the prior steps you've no doubt identified some of the tasks, so you have a head start.

This chapter may seem more straightforward because the ideas are fundamental to project management and are probably familiar at some level. To those readers who have been breathlessly waiting to crank up your project management software, let 'er rip. Software works wonders with Inputs. You can now lay out a coherent task list with greater confidence that you are aiming at the right set of well-tuned Outcomes.

The LogFrame Inputs are not meant to offer a detailed action plan, simply a first cut or high level summary. LogFrame Inputs are the jumping off point for more precise planning using Work Breakdown Structures (WBS), Gantt Charts, networks and so forth. You can identify a few illustrative Input activities in your LogFrame to use as a starting point, then develop a more detailed work plan using Microsoft Project® or similar tools. You can later paste a reasonably accurate high level summary of that detailed work plan back into your LogFrame's Input row.

Chunk Out By Phase/Element

For a major, long-term project with multiple phases and chunks, Input planning may first involve roughing out a general schedule of future phases. This is what the OSRP group did with a simple multi-year Gantt chart, as shown below.

OSRP Timeline

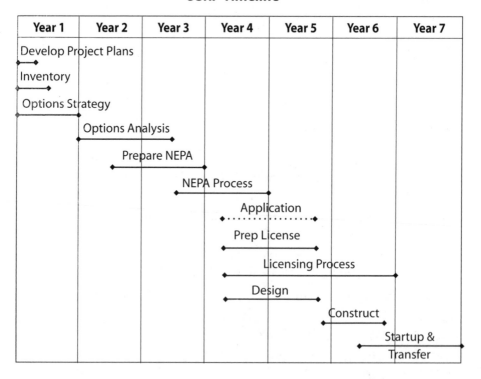

Year 1	Year 2	Year 3	Year 4	Year 5	Year 6	Year 7
Develop Project Plans						
Inventory						
Options Strategy						
	Options Analysis					
	Prepare NEPA					
		NEPA Process				
			Application			
			Prep License			
			Licensing Process			
			Design			
				Construct		
					Startup & Transfer	

Applying Schmidt's Law

Recall that during the chunking discussion in Chapter Four, I stressed the importance of breaking your project into logical and named phases. Each phase deserves its own LogFrame. When you're planning for the current phase, you must also anticipate future phases. *Schmidt's Law of Planning Density* recommends that you plan the upcoming phase/chunk at the level of detail you need to manage it effectively, and simultaneously create less detailed preliminary plans for subsequent phases.

For simplicity, let's assume that you have a one-year project with four phases of three months each. *Schmidt's Law* specifies that subsequent phases Two, Three and Four should have roughly 1/2, 1/3, and 1/4 the level of detail as Phase One. If, for example, Phase One is a three-month effort with 25 action items, your preliminary plans for the next three phases would have roughly 12, 8, and 4 action items, respectively. A graphic depiction of this concept follows:

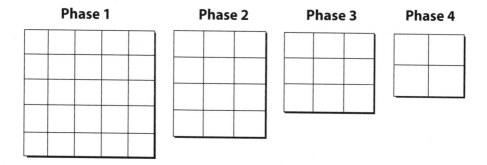

Phase 1   **Phase 2**   **Phase 3**   **Phase 4**

Preliminary plans for future phases will have much less granularity and specificity than for your current phase, but enough detail to spot long-lead items and future issues with present action implications.

Each phase will have its own LogFrame, with phase-specific Purpose and Outcomes, but all phases will share a common, over-arching goal.

You can create preliminary plans for future phases as separate LogFrames or incorporate them into your current phase LogFrame. For example, the last Outcome on a LogFrame for any phase could be "Preliminary Plans for Later Phases Developed."

Defining Inputs: Action Steps and Resources

Inputs are defined as the activities or tasks needed to produce Outcomes and the resources that they require. In any undertaking, the three major resources of interest are people, time, and assets (money and the things money can buy, i.e., equipment, facilities, materials). A well-partitioned (chunked) activity list is the starting point for identifying the resources needed for each and estimating Outcome costs.

Here's an excerpt showing Outcome #3 from the Fircrest School LogFrame found in the Appendix. Note the appropriate density of the Input activity planning: descriptive but not overwhelming.

Outcome 3: Quality Assurance System Implemented

Input Activities	Responsibility	Resources		Schedule
		$	**Human Resources (person - weeks)**	
1.1 Assign staff	Superintendent			~~~
1.2 Design system	Expert	$25K	4	~~~
1.3 Purchase computers	Bus. manager	$5 -10K	1	~~~
1.4 Create prototype	QA Team	-	3	~~~
1.5 Collect QA data	QA Team	-	3	~~~
1.6 Distribute QA data	QA Team		1	~~~
	Total	$ 30-40 K	12 person-weeks	

Break each Outcome down into a set of clear, delegable, actionable tasks. As a rule of thumb, limit your activities to four to seven per Outcome. These chunk sizes keep you from being overwhelmed with detail. Of course, you can go to any level of granularity you wish, using a WBS, a separate list, or your tool of choice.

By definition, an activity takes time and consumes resources. Inputs and activities are the action steps needed to produce each Outcome. Outcomes mark the completion of a series of activities. List Inputs using a numbering convention which links them to their respective Outcome, as shown in the Fircrest LogFrame.

Note that some of the tasks for Outcome #3 are large enough to justify their own LogFrame. Activity 3.2, "Design System," is clearly a project in itself. While it is condensed to an Input on this Master LogFrame, the expert in charge created a spin-off LogFrame for system design.

One of the LogFrame's many useful features is its ability to loosely couple together several LogFrames as "linked clusters." Linked clusters group together separate LogFrames which work together toward a common Goal. These linked LogFrames might, for example, flesh out parallel interface projects, address setting up the Purpose level Verification mechanisms, or handle a key Assumption.

The ability to bundle multiple LogFrames around themes which cut across separate organization units can be very potent.

Inputs vs. Outcomes

Confusion may pop up in the relationship between activities and Outcomes. Take, for example, "develop system." Is this an Input activity or an Outcome? The answer is, it could be both.

As grammatically stated, it's clearly an activity. But if you are responsible to deliver a developed system, then it becomes an Outcome and should be restated in past-tense language that describes what it looks like when it is complete. The reason for this is simple. The human brain can more easily describe what something looks, smells, and tastes like if it is visualized as being a completed result ("_____ed").

So, let me spell it out further.

Outcome	1. System **Developed**
Inputs	1. **Develop** System

The statement "if we develop system, then system is developed" is true but simplistic and not too helpful. The power comes when you then explode or break out the activity "develop system" into its component parts, like so:

Outcome	1. System Developed
Inputs	1.1 Identify requirements
	1.2 Write specifications
	1.3 Develop new system
	1.4 Test system

Now these four tasks can be further broken down into sub-tasks, or they can be elevated to Outcome milestones. During initial project brainstorming, you'll come up with a mixed list of Objectives, some of which will end up as Outcomes, and others as Inputs, with the rest tossed aside. Make sure to convert those Objectives you select to make Outcomes into Outcome language, and then develop an appropriate list of supporting Inputs. Done well, this entails interactive and dynamic thinking at its best, as you refine the Outcome set into a well-chunked and logically derived scope.

Crystallize Which Tasks Need Doing, and When

Having specified key activities, you can then identify preceding and succeeding tasks, sequence them, and rough out a provisional schedule using a Gantt chart, network, or some similar tool. This first-pass time-line is subject to later revision, but it's good enough to peg the start times and durations of the various activities required to achieve the stated Outcomes. There's no need for me to delve deeply into the details of task planning here, because there are plenty of good materials available on that topic.

Building The World's Longest Bar Chart

Speaking of Gannt charts, the very first one I ever encountered should be listed in the Guinness Book of World Records. A dubious accomplishment from my college days, I built the world's longest bar chart!

As an aerospace engineering sophomore at the University of Washington in Seattle, I needed a part-time job. Boeing advertised a "hands-on" role setting up the scheduling system for the very first Boeing 747, when project management software was still in its infancy. It sounded simple enough and I was ready to play a role in building this ground-breaking aircraft.

The true meaning of "hands-on" became clear on the first day when they handed me a box of 1/4" thick black artists' tape and told me that my job was to install the grid lines on a mile-long Formica wall in a tunnel under Boeing's facility in Everett, WA. I'm not exaggerating when I say it was a mile long. The Everett Boeing plant is one of the world's largest buildings and home of the first 747. You can fit all of Disneyland inside the building!

The top line had to be six feet high, so I stood on tip toes to tape the top parallel line and worked horizontally across a mile. Then I'd drop down six inches and tape together another mile-long line. The bottom few rows required that I crawl on the floor, but I didn't care. This was my first ever hands-on system installation project and I was amped!

Much to the relief of my aching back, a few days later it was time to paste in the vertical grid lines, spaced a foot apart, one for each day leading to aircraft rollout. Then the engineers began to populate the cells of my gigantic grid. Into the cells went blocks of text identifying tasks and vendors on the critical path for integrating all the aircraft components and making them available to the entire Boeing 747 team.

I felt proud as a pup with a new collar upon arriving at work each afternoon after calculus class, and watching the first fuselage being assembled. The concentric circle ribbing looked like the skeleton of a giant dinosaur. But I enjoyed only a brief glance at the end results of my work enroute to my "system installation" job down deep in the tunnel. Since then, my appreciation for software that does the task-management legwork has skyrocketed, while my discomfort around rolls of black tape remains.

Choose Meaningful Milestones

If you were to drive from San Francisco's Golden Gate all the way to New York's Statue of Liberty, you could search frantically for every milepost, telephone pole, and center-line dash along the way, evidence of forward motion toward your New York goal. Or you could accept Salt Lake City, Chicago and, say, Pittsburgh or Cleveland as reasonable milestones on your journey. In this world of too much information, it's easy to get lost in details. Set your focus on significant milestones and be judicious in selecting those primary project checkpoints. Make milestones meaningful.

What justifies being called a milestone? Whatever makes the best progress markers. Outcome completion is an automatic milestone, but the start or completion of key activities, Assumptions verification, and mid-project reviews may also constitute milestones.

How many milestones? Schmidt's Law suggests that a six-month project usually needs somewhere around 12 to 15 milestone points, or one every two weeks or so. A one-month project might have one or two milestones per week. On longer projects, avoid going more than three weeks between milestones or people may lose focus.

Reaching Your Milestones On-Time

Sometimes it's wise to insert early "trip-wire" points a week ahead of a milestone's due date to provide an early-warning status check. This recognizes the natural human tendency among most people (myself included) to wait until it's very late in the game to get started. I'm not alone in remembering certain college term papers that a professor assigned two months previously, and that I would wait until a few nights before the due date to start working on it, maybe pulling an all-nighter to finish. The papers passed but they were not my best work. Can you also identify with "term-paper syndrome"?

My favorite aerospace engineering professor, Reiner Decher, did his class a great favor (and taught a project management lesson) by requiring a thorough outline be submitted three weeks in advance of the term paper due date. This forced an earlier start, which resulted in a better final product.

Take time to acknowledge on-time performance when your team does reach their milestone targets. Remember, you're working with fellow humans who could really appreciate an "Atta-girl" or "Atta-boy" for making their milestones on time. Sure, they're getting paid, but if you give public kudos and recognition when they hit the mark, they'll give their best to hit their other targets too.

Clarify Resource Needs

To reiterate a key point, the main resources categorize into people, time, and assets (i.e., money and the things money can buy: equipment, facilities, and materials). The LogFrame structure permits great flexibility in how you do resource planning. Feel free to tailor the formats to match the resource categories that are most relevant to your project or most helpful in your planning. When your organization tracks time against projects, contracts or clients, use the relevant categories and accounting codes.

To develop your project budget, identify and then cost out all of the resources needed for each activity necessary to produce the stated Outcomes.

With reasonably good estimates at the activity/Input level, you will end up with a defensible budget that shows what it will take to deliver your defined Outcomes. The more precision you demonstrate, the better. It will inoculate you (somewhat) against project budget cuts, because you can more easily trace back the impact of these cuts on the project.

Make Roles and Responsibilities Crystal Clear

The Saga of the Confused Project Team

Four people named Everybody, Somebody, Anybody and Nobody worked together. An important Outcome needed managing, and Everybody was sure that Somebody would do it. Anybody could have done it, but Nobody actually did it. Somebody got angry, because it was really Everybody's job. Everybody thought Anybody could do it, but Nobody realized that Somebody wouldn't. As it turned out, Everybody blamed Somebody when Nobody did what Anybody could have done!

Sound familiar? Blame, wasted effort, and sour feelings occur when something drops through the cracks due to poor communication or faulty coordination. Sorting out roles and responsibilities is tricky because most tasks involve multiple people. Fortunately, there's a simple tool to assist us: The Linear Responsibility Chart. The Linear Responsibility Chart identifies project "actions" (tasks or activities) and "actors" (organizations/individuals) in a matrix that shows:

- All persons or organizations involved in the project (along the horizontal line)
- All tasks or activities (along the vertical line)
- The nature of the involvement of all persons in the project task (by code in the matrix).

Use this simple letter code to identify the responsibilities of each player:

R: Responsible for the action (but may delegate)

P: Participates in the action

C: May be consulted

A: Must approve

I: Must be informed

The example on the next page is from the Caribbean Agriculture Research and Development Institute (CARDI), a 13-nation consortium of small island nations that pool their limited technical resources to tackle problems of common interest. Key players in this chart include both internal and external parties who were involved in creating their annual R&D plans. External actors are the various government Ministries of Agriculture from participating countries, while internal actors are the individual groups most directly involved. Note how responsibility shifts by activity, and that some involve dual levels of approval.

Clarify Roles & Responsibilities

(CARDI – Caribbean Agriculture Research & Development Institute)

Code:
R = Responsible to do
P = Participates in doing
C = May be consulted
I = Must be informed
A = Approves

PROJECT OUTCOME:
CARDI R & D PLAN DEVELOPED

Activities	CARDI INTERNAL					EXTERNAL		
	Board of Gov.	Exec Dir.	R & D Dir.	Budget Dir.	Research Teams	Jamaica Gov.	Barbados Govt.	Belize Govt.
1. Evaluate Prior Year Results		I	R		P	C	C	C
2. Clarify Research Objectives		A	R	P	P	C	C	C
3. Set R&D Priorities	I	R	P	P	P	C	C	C
4. Establish Budget levels	R	P	P	P	P			
5. Prepare Preliminary Project Proposals		I	A	C	R	P	P	P
6. Review and Rank All Proposals		A	R	C	P			
7. Choose PRoposals to Fund		A	R	P	I	C	C	C
8. Prepare Final Plan/Budget	A2	A1	R	P	C			
9. Publish & Communicate Plan	I	R	P	P	P	I	I	I

How to Construct a Responsibility Chart

Ideally, get your key players together in front of a large whiteboard. Alternately, one or two people can develop and circulate the chart (stamped 'draft') to others for review. Have your LogFrame available as a starting point. Follow these steps:

1. Clarify the Outcome or task of interest.

2. Draw a large matrix on the blackboard or whiteboard.

3. List all the activities vertically; list key actors horizontally (leave some blank columns).

4. Discuss each activity and define roles with a letter code.

The team discussions around task roles frequently leads to a redefinition or finer–grained breakouts of tasks. For example, "purchase hardware" may break out into "finalize specs," "identify possible vendors," "invite bids," "select hardware," etc.

While you can have more than one person participate (P), Approve (A), Consult (C), or be Informed (I), only one person should wear the Responsibility hat (R). The responsible person can delegate, of course, and the people delegated would be labeled with a "P", but it is imperative that every action has an "R," i.e., someone responsible for the action.

Having multiple R's for a single task diffuses accountability and invites finger-pointing.

Responsibility charts can easily be turned into job descriptions by reading each column vertically and putting the contents into standard narrative format for distribution among the project staff.

Hybrid Input Formats

Be creative in adapting the LogFrame to your team's needs. Feel free to add your own project-useful categories at the Input level. One such hybrid format follows. Note the addition of two columns on the right that capture the information needed and its source. Rather than displaying a full Responsibility Chart, this LogFrame variation simply identifies who is responsible and lumps all other actors into an "others involved category" next to the "R."

Input Activities	Primary Responsibility	Others Involved	Complete By When	Resources Required	Information Needed	Information Source
1.1						
1.2						
1.3						
etc.						

The Value of Defining the Next Step

Do you find it easy to procrastinate on key tasks because they seem so big or are still somewhat fuzzy? Do you sometimes want to move ahead, but aren't sure what your next step is? Your mind can play tricks on you and bombard you with innumerable reasons to put things off.

A professional colleague and master of elegant execution, David Allen, taught me how to solve that problem. He shares this next tip in his book, *Getting Things Done*, paraphrased here.

"Define the next action step" is a success principle that has proven itself enormously valuable. For example, confronting a task like "Improve Marketing Strategy" can lead to getting overwhelmed or stuck because you can clearly see several tasks within the task. So, it starts to look huge every time you try to get started on it.

What is the solution? Define the next discrete, doable step that you can take. What is it? "Review the present plan?" "Locate the present plan under other stuff on your desk?" "Retrieve the plan from the circular file?" Then, define the next action step, i.e., "Read old plan." What then? "Highlight good parts in yellow." And then, oh, "Find yellow highlighter."

By breaking your task into discrete packets at this level of granularity, you effectively defuse your fear by showing yourself that the big scary task is actually a series of small, simple, tasks! You don't need to go atomic on your "What do I do next?" breakdown. Just take it to the level where you can envision yourself doing those necessary, important, mostly ordinary tasks that effective humans do to get things done. Some of the most productive next steps might be to:

- Visit or call someone on the phone.

- Send someone an email.

- Locate a document on your computer.

- Do an online search to research some question.

- Make a decision (about what you researched).

- Create a new electronic file and brainstorm some ideas.

To make your actions productive, ask whether or not there is still some prior step to be done in preparation for the meeting, phone call, or email, such as getting some missing information. Be prepared.

That is your real next step! Take it now, and take your next step after that, and then the next, and soon you'll be river dancing yourself, and your team, into a flow of true project productivity. There's a psychological lift from getting into this "flow state" because breaking seemingly insurmountable tasks into sure-thing next steps builds inner strength and momentum.

Key Points Review

1. LogFrame Inputs can be illustrative and not definitive. They are simply the starting points for more detailed planning using other task management tools.

2. Activities are different than Outcomes. By definition, an activity consumes time and requires resources – human and other. Activities are the action steps needed to produce each Outcome, while Outcomes mark the completion of a series of activities.

3. Clear responsibility paves the way for coordinated execution. Use Responsibility Charts to define and agree on responsibility and authority issues. Developing the chart as a team provides a way to sort out potential coordination difficulties in advance.

4. Remember the "next action step" principle and break down tasks into the very next action you need to take.

5. Like the law of gravity, Schmidt's Law of Planning Density is more than a law, it's also a good idea.

Application Step #4:

At this point you can use software or continue with old-fashioned technology – pencils!

1. Confirm the Outcomes. Affirm that they are our best guess as to the "necessary and sufficient" set needed to reach the Purpose.

2. List key activities for each Outcome, chunked out at roughly the same level of detail. Begin each with a verb and number them to correspond to their related Outcomes. Limit your activities to four to seven per outcome, so you don't get overwhelmed.

3. Identify task sequences by examining predecessor or successor events.

4. Identify resources needed for each task.

5. Develop Gantt chart or similar task schedule.

6. Clarify responsibilities; use the Responsibility Chart.

If you've been applying the action steps at the ends of Chapters 4-7 to your project, you have now fleshed out a first draft LogFrame. In the Appendix you'll find a self-administering quality-checklist that you can use to determine how well your project design hangs together. Use this to spot and correct weaknesses. After cleaning up your design, circulate it to a few key players for some live feedback.

Note: You can create a LogFrame grid in Excel or Microsoft Word, and you can also check out *www.ManagementPro.com* for templates and support tools.

Part Three:
Putting the Concepts Into Action

Previous chapters guided you in creating a sound project plan, guided by the four critical strategic questions and using the LogFrame structure. A sound plan is necessary for success, but it is not, by itself, sufficient.

These three chapters cover other critical issues for putting your LogFrame to work and getting the results you seek.

Chapter Eight explores ways to manage the dynamics of teams and stakeholders.

Chapter Nine examines how to execute and update your plans using the Action Learning Cycle.

Chapter Ten illustrates a dozen typical high-payoff applications, and offers tips for getting started.

Chapter 8: Managing the People Dynamics

"If we don't worry about who gets the credit,
just think how much we can accomplish"
– Ronald Reagan

The Heart and Soul of Projects

We sometimes equate project management with the visible planning artifacts – timelines, budgets, and reports. But the heart and soul of every project concerns people – their relationships, skills, and ability to work as a team. Shrewd project managers focus their attention from day one on understanding the human dynamics of every project step, and even anticipate probable human interactions as the project unfolds.

Putting people first multiplies your odds of success. Consider this key premise: *How you develop a project plan and who you involve is as important as the actual plan itself.* People who perceive themselves as co-creators of a vision are more positively involved and committed. The challenge lies in getting that critical "buy-in" and maintaining "stay-in."

Engaging Your Key Stakeholders

Paul Newman, playing an aging pool hustler in the movie *The Color of Money*, revealed his secret of success to his protégé, played by Tom Cruise. "I'm a student of human moves." Becoming a master student of human moves is a psychologically dynamic project in and of itself, and is a critical skill for any successful project leader. Understanding people's interests, nurturing relationships, and building a supporting coalition is as important as managing tasks on the Gantt chart.

The people dimension emphasizes relative relationships with two often-overlapping groups: key stakeholders and team members. Do your initial stakeholder analysis early and update it often as the project evolves. Begin by identifying the spectrum of possible stakeholders whom the project affects, involves, or concerns. Ask yourself the following questions:

1. Who are we doing this for? (customers or end-users)

2. Who really wants to see this happen? (champions)

3. Who might be opposed? (blockers)

4. Who else is affected? (indirect beneficiaries and/or victims)

5. Whose support or assistance do we need to execute the project? (cooperators and implementers)

6. What resources do we need, and who controls them? (gatekeepers and enablers)

7. Who is paying for this? (sponsors)

Analyze Stakeholder Interests

Stakeholder analysis yields the most accurate insights when done by the core team, with input from champions. Using my favorite tool, a large whiteboard, sketch a simple matrix and list the major players vertically. Then identify, as best you can, their major interests, and issues concerning the effort.

Next, identify the degree of support you *need* from each stakeholder, and the degree of support you *predict* you will have. Then you can decide how best to involve them in the initial planning and in subsequent stages.

Stakeholder	Interests & Issues	Degree of Support Needed			Degree of Support Predicted		
		Crucial	Somewhat	Not Needed	Strong	Neutral	Opposed

Look for gaps between the support you need and the support you predict you will have. If a stakeholder's support is crucial, or somewhat important, and you predict neutral support or outright opposition, figure out what you might do to get their backing. Some options include:

- **Enroll them** – Get them enthused about the vision.

- **Convince them** – Use reasoned discourse.

- **Accommodate them** – Incorporate their interests in your solution.

- **Trade them** – Commit to "owing them" one in the future.

- **Pressure them** – Use legitimate power to reduce resistance.

- **Love them** – Use your personality to smother them in good will.

If these approaches don't work, your remaining options are to:

- **Moot them** – Make them irrelevant by insulating the project from their non-support.

- **Ignore them** – Acknowledge their concerns but press ahead anyway.

A stakeholder analysis for small projects can be handled with tools as simple as a pencil, some paper, and a few moments of time. Big projects may need many days of intense, thought-provoking sessions, during which several people are phoning, emailing, meeting and listening to all those who hold a stake, one way or another, in the project.

Consider this example from the Asian Gypsy Moth project, formed to combat a major pest invasion that threatened to destroy the forests of the Pacific Northwest. Combating the pest invasion began with helicopter spraying 40,000 acres in and around Seattle, using a non-toxic biological pesticide. After the spraying, the team had to deploy and check 180,000 traps for several months. This quick-response project grew from a staff of just 3 to 300 people in just 8 weeks! The project's people dynamics and issues were substantial!

Review the project's stakeholder analysis matrix, shown as an example on the next page.

Stakeholders Analysis Matrix – Asian Gypsy Moth Invasion

Stakeholder	Interests & Issues	Degree of Support Needed			Degree of Support Predicted		
		Crucial	Some-what	Not Needed	Strong	Neutral	Opposed
1. Governor's Office	Minimize active public opposition	X			X		
2. Legislators	Represent constituent interests. Visible active oversight	X				X	
3. Dept. of Health	Ensure safety and health		X			X	
4. Agriculture Industry	Minimize costs to farmers	X			X	X	
5. WSDA Personnel Dept	Hire necessary staff	X				X	
6. Ecologists	Restore healthy interaction webs. Minimize "collateral" damage to non-target species		X				
7. Buttery collectors	Minimize "collateral" damage to non-target species		X				X
8. General Public	Be safe	X					X
9. Media	Inform the public	X				X	
10. Moths	Survive!			X			X

The Governor was fully supportive, along with the timber and agriculture industry. Ecologists, eco-activists and environmentalists, who could potentially have stopped the project, were generally united in their desire to rid the beautiful northwest of a truly dangerous pest using proven natural predators, rather than damaging insecticides.

But several troubling gaps appeared in the stakeholder chart. Note that legislator support (stakeholder #2) was crucial, but initially predicted as neutral because they did not yet understand the project Objectives and the urgency. This pinpointed a need to brief them personally and win their active support. Big gaps between needed and predicted support showed up with the general public.

The general public's support (#8) was vital since low-flying helicopters would soon be buzzing their neighborhoods spraying a mysterious mist. Special efforts were required to educate the public. Media cooperation was essential to get a fair warning out to the citizens about the seriousness of the problem, while not triggering a panic. Butterfly collectors, a politically influential group, initially opposed the effort but lent support after the project team added funds to restock the butterfly population.

This analysis revealed that the only stakeholders strongly opposed to the effort were the moths themselves. Fortunately, their support was not needed.

Building Your Own Dream Team

When the 1980 U.S. Olympic Hockey Team beat the Russians, the whole world was shocked. How could a bunch of amateur college players whip a seasoned professional Russian team? If you saw the movie *Miracle*, you'll remember that dramatic moment when the twenty U.S. hockey players jelled to become a team, not just a collection of individuals.

Harmonizing the efforts and energies of the team is so much more than courtesy or politically correct maneuvering. Hold in your mind the image of a six-cylinder engine firing on all cylinders, but badly out of timing. Misaligned cylinders use their strength against each other, and the leftover energy is barely enough to move the car. Setting the timing, gapping the plugs, and ensuring a close fit on the valves is analogous to harmonizing a project team. With some conscious attention, the various components are honed and fitted to work with each other to build forward momentum, instead of against each other or simply at random.

A valuable secondary benefit accrues when teams use the LogFrame. Powerful team-building occurs during the process. The LogFrame, by requiring a disciplined and interactive dialogue involving all players, quickly highlights issues, helps members discover and eliminate ignorant spots, and facilitates inter-player cooperation. The bottom line: better projects and committed teams.

Start With Your Core Team

Core team members are your backbone – the trusted team members needed to get the ball rolling and keep it rolling. They are usually not the high rollers or champions, but the prime doers. Who are these people? Are they committed? Do they bring the right resources – technical, interpersonal, and emotional – needed to help produce spectacular results? You don't need to identify every team member at once, but you'd better find a few sparkplugs early on. Here are some questions to ask, as you ponder the composition of your team:

1. What technical skills do we need to get the job done, and who has them?

2. What other skills or perspectives do we need, and who has them?

3. Who would it be smart to include for political reasons?

4. Whose involvement would give the project greater credibility and visibility?

5. Who gives us access to information and other resources?

6. For each potential person, what's their track record as a team player?

You may be assigned people or need to beat the bushes to recruit team members. Either way, make sure you understand the following critical concept.

Yes, It's All About Me!

Let's face it: we all have psychological needs we seek to satisfy. Everyone is super-busy, and your target team members are probably already overextended, and therefore, unable or unwilling to take on your project. They may not be thrilled at being recruited, so you must appeal to individual human needs and answer the primary question swirling in each of their minds: **What's in it for me? (WIIFM)**.

What can serving on your project offer each team member? Figure out people's hot buttons and communicate how your project can fulfill their desire to:

- Work on challenging problems

- Be recognized and visible

- Learn, grow, and gain new skills

- Apply their core expertise

- Experience variety and stimulation

- Accomplish something important

- Get tangible rewards (e.g., bonuses)

- Work with new people in different parts of the organization

- Have fun

While we're on the subject, be sure to figure out your own personal WIIFM. Motivating yourself is even more essential than motivating others, especially when your project runs for a long time. No one stays energized and focused all the time, so you'll find your time well-invested when you remind yourself of the many payoffs in it for *you*.

Size Matters

How large should the core team be? That depends on the project's size and complexity. Avoid making it so large that it becomes cumbersome, or so small that it fails to include diverse perspectives. My experience suggests that the ideal size is between five to seven persons (plus or minus two). This group size is optimum for active give-and-take discussions.

When a core team has between nine and fifteen people, it becomes more of a committee than a team, and the expression "nothing ever gets done in a committee" often proves true. If you are forced to include a large number of people, take extra care that the group is extremely well-structured, or it can become a well-meaning but unruly mob. The larger the number, the more important it is to engage a neutral external facilitator in conducting the initial meetings so you start on a solid footing.

Team dynamics must gel. You are not just recruiting good individuals, but good individuals who will function well as a team. Shaquille O'Neal and Kobe Bryant are both exceptional basketball players, individually, but fouled up and fouled out when playing together. Good team play beats gifted individual stars, every time.

Seven people with key operational roles made up the core Asian Gypsy Moth team. Over the project's first two months, the project team grew to nearly 300 people as field teams were deployed. But like a human pyramid of cheerleaders stacked five persons high, the stability of the project structure depended on the core team serving as a strong and solid base.

You can't always get the right people. Your best efforts may produce a team, but not the team you really want to work with. In the final analysis, if you've exhausted all other selection and recruiting tactics, and you've done as much persuasive enrolling as possible, then accept the people on your team, and realize that there's plenty of opportunity to make it a success. Accept them for who they are, and who they are not, then busy yourself equipping them with the necessary tools and common language to execute the project.

You can complain about the availability or non-availability of "the right people" until your window of opportunity has long since slammed shut, or you can turn your people into the right people. Put your faith in those you have. Transform the people you have into the people you need!

When You Serve on the Core Team

When you are asked to be part of a project team, you owe it to yourself to take a few moments and think through your own role in the grand scheme of the project. Questions that can help you sort out your commitment include:

- Just why do they want me?

- What role would I like to have?

- What might this role develop into?

- Why me? What do I bring to the project?

- What's in it for me?

- What do I have to give up to be involved in this?

Be sure your conscience is clear so you can commit with all you've got. A halting, on-again/off-again approach – being neither slow nor fast – usually ends up half-fast and does everyone involved a disservice. Be able to commit completely to bring all of your talents to the table, to bear down on the project, as if you personally owned it. You do own it!

When you and other team members move with swift certitude, conviction, and clarity of Purpose, your team will become an unstoppable force.

Creating Shared Norms for High Performance

The need for shared norms and guiding principles (or "rules of the game") may be obvious to you. But other team members, support staff, or secondary enablers may not think it's all that necessary. Therefore, take steps to discuss this early in the process. Norms must be deliberately shaped. If left to chance, inefficient practices and dysfunctional behavior can quickly become acceptable standards.

The OSRP sealed source team developed norms which promoted operational efficiency. These included:

- When we disagree, we attack the issue, not the person.

- We respect, honor and support each other.

- We acknowledge good ideas and creative contributions from all.

- We all do our job and deliver products on time.

- We begin each meeting by defining expectations and Outcomes, and by reviewing decisions and action items.

- We self-monitor to make sure we are all contributing value.

Team chemistry can make or break a project, so it's worth your time and effort to build the right expectations from day one.

On this project, "John" was a technically superb but long-winded task force member who frequently talked about experiences and situations totally outside the team meetings' agendas. But the other team players deferred to and respected his expertise, so they were reluctant to interrupt his meandering monologues.

The team leader approached John privately and acknowledged his valuable input while pointing out that the extraneous conversation was annoying and counterproductive. "Could you help me break this habit?" John asked, and the team leader assured him of his help.

At the next project meeting, the team leader explained that, as a team leader, he sometimes talked too long, so if he (or others on team) were getting too talkative, they had permission to set "these" into action, He then handed out a set of wind-up mechanical chattering teeth to each team member! With help from the clattering of insistent incisors, John quickly learned to cut short his off-topic spoken strolls, and did so with a chuckle.

Grow Your Own Norms

No single list of best-practice norms works in every context. Take the list above as a starting point and add to it. Better yet, start from scratch and "grow your own," based on an open discussion of principles that have made past projects successful.

When Hewlett Packard project leader Joe Cronin kicks off new project teams, he shares some of the flub-ups from his early career days, and thus develops rapport with the group. He also asks each person to describe their most successful and satisfying projects, and then has the group distill a common set of best-practice principles to apply in the project at hand.

Getting all team members focused on what makes for good teamwork leads to the definition of good teamwork, the practice of good teamwork, and the benefits of good teamwork. Norm-setting is a great foundation to quickly cement friendships, enhance professional respect and promote *esprit de corps* among what would otherwise be polite strangers.

People thrive on challenges, overcoming obstacles, winning against the odds and doing an exceptionally good job. Call your team to the harmony of excellence, and enjoy the "tabernacle choir" sounds of their harmonized efforts.

Making Meetings March Along

Meetings can become a time sucking swamp for all because it's so easy to get side-tracked or spend excess time on minor issues. One team burdened by excessively long discussions of technical issues adopted the following protocols to close an issue and move on. They agreed that when things bogged down, the project manager could end discussion on a topic with any one of these statements:

- **"I've got it."** Enough! We understand the issues, now let's move on to the next item.

- **"We'll revisit it later."** Table it for now, but decide *when* to revisit it.

- **"We need more information."** Assign someone to write up the issue or do research.

- **"Let's summarize and move on."** Summarize the agreement or decision we made and proceed.

- **"Important topic, but not at this time".** Note it, and pick it up at some later time (decide when).

- **"Our next steps are."** Agree on an action and by-when date for someone.

The most important protocol to keep meetings on-track is to clarify expected meeting Objectives at the start. The agenda item may read "discuss topic" but the real Objective is "make a decision concerning." Another best-practice protocol to build accountability is to have all persons recap their action responsibilities and due dates at the meeting's end.

Sharpening Your Emotional Intelligence

Bring to mind the most effective project managers you have ever encountered. Chances are that they have strong Emotional Intelligence skills, in addition to their technical and project management skills. Emotional Intelligence (EI) simply means being strategic and intentional in using your emotions – and those of others – to achieve project objectives.

EI matters because project management requires that you achieve results through others. This means being able to build trust, handle conflict, give and take criticism constructively, deal with people who don't deliver, generate team commitment, and keep yourself and others motivated over the long haul. Skillfully handling situations like this means tapping into an innate capacity that we all have – our Emotional Intelligence – but few fully develop.

EI is not about suppressing or denying your emotions, it's about recognizing the signals they give you, learning from them, then being willing to manage and control them. When you are disappointed, for example, it does no good to deny that feeling, but it is valuable to understand the message behind the disappointment, which is the sense of being let down.

Emotional Intelligence gives you the edge in projects and in life. Sharpening your EI means developing yourself in four major domains:

1. **High self-awareness.** This is the ability to tune into yourself, self-monitor in real time, see the impact of your behavior, and fine-tune your approach to get the results you want. High self-awareness begins with listening to how you talk to yourself. By becoming more mindful about how your inner dialogues shape your feelings, actions, and reactions, you can work to change any self-defeating thought patterns.

2. **Mood Management.** Learn to manage your moods and choose the most productive ones to be effective now. Recognize that it's not the event that causes you to feel good or bad; rather, it's how you appraise the event that determines your emotional reaction. When emotions such as anger and anxiety come up, what counts is how

skillfully and swiftly you can move out of those debilitating states to more productive ones. Practice paying attention to the specific statements you make to yourself when you are emotionally aggravated or distressed. Remind yourself to talk to yourself in ways that help you manage your emotions, instead of letting your emotions manage you.

3. **Self-motivation.** The best leaders can jump-start themselves into action, and stay focused on what's most important now. Self-motivation keeps you energized, reduces emotional swings, and helps you bounce back quickly from setbacks. Spark your motivation by constructing motivating instructional self-statements to remind you that you have the knowledge, skills, and drive to get a particular task done. Create positive pep-talks to give to yourself… "I can do this marketing plan. I've fully researched all the issues. No one understands the marketplace as I do. No matter what, I will prepare an outstanding plan."

Inoculate yourself against future difficulties by writing instructional self-statements in advance. What are some potentially difficult situations you might face when dealing with customers, clients, and team members? What instructional self-statements could you create now that would help you sail smoothly through future storms?

4. **Interpersonal expertise.** This is the ability to handle the inevitable conflicts, disagreements and criticisms that crop up in all projects. Strong interpersonal expertise lets you respond effectively to team members and stakeholders, no matter how negative their emotional states might be. Strong interpersonal expertise equips you to help other people deal with their emotions, resolve their conflicts, and stay productive.

Ten Techniques for Increasing Your Emotional Intelligence

In our forthcoming book, *Emotional Intelligence for Project Managers,* Dr. Hendrie Weisinger (author of *Emotional Intelligence at Work*) and I identify ten techniques you can use. One of the simplest techniques is to *generate humor.*

Successful project managers must be able to attract people and create a positive atmosphere. Humor is a fun way to do this. From a scientific point of view, laughing releases endorphins – hormones and enzymes that make you feel good – as well as help you relax, and even heal.

Having a sense of humor means being able to sense when humor is appropriate because the intent of humor is not to embarrass or humiliate people, but to make them laugh and dispel tension. A practical rule of thumb is to ask yourself if the joke you plan to tell could offend somebody. If the answer is *yes*, or *maybe*, better choose another.

To work humor into your projects, start the ritual of beginning team meetings with a joke or two. Open the next meeting with jokes of your own. Then ask for volunteers to prepare a joke for the next meeting.

There are still plenty of jokes around that will generate hearty laughter, even in these politically correct times. The World Wide Web is a rich source. Google search for terms like "project management humor" or "management jokes." The very best form of humor is self-deprecating humor, where you make yourself the butt of the joke.

Can you see how Emotional Intelligence and the Logical Framework fit together? Smoothly functioning projects require that the manager and team are emotionally intelligent, which would show up in the Assumptions column. The emotionally unintelligent manager who, for example, criticizes a team member so harshly that he damages his or her spirit, will have a tough time delivering Outcomes.

When guiding a team in crafting their project LogFrame, I'll sometimes suggest adding the Assumption that "the project team will perform in an emotionally intelligent manner." This catalyzes the team conversation about what Emotional Intelligence means in their context, and the behaviors it will take to make that Assumption valid.

Develop a Start-Up LogFrame

Experienced project managers understand that team selection and team formation are crucial parts of any successful project. Whether team members have been recruited, selected, or appointed, the way that the initial team *comes together* and gels (or doesn't) will have a significant impact on their performance throughout the life of the project.

Once the team has come together and has been adequately informed of the parameters of their mission (should they choose to accept it), an outstanding way to get them rapidly focused and moving ahead is to have them prepare a LogFrame of the *project system*. A start-up LogFrame is broader than your project-focused LogFrame (the project-focused LogFrame appears as one of several Outcomes on the start-up matrix). This broader LogFrame typically addresses general project preparation and structure decisions, such as:

- What is our target date for completing our project design?

- Which key stakeholders should we involve in initial planning? By when should we make this decision and invite their involvement?

- Do we need additional project team members?

- What processes, systems, and tools will we use for the project? Who will manage them?

- How, and how often, will we monitor our progress on the project?

- To whom should we report project progress? What reporting tools should we use?

Rather than leave these decisions to chance, or solely to the project manager, use them as an opportunity to involve the team from the get-go. Developing a start-up LogFrame will also familiarize the team with the LogFrame model concept, encouraging them to use it to think through and plan more than just the project itself. This action, done soon after the team is formed, can transform the team into a high-caliber crew, with all the requisite attitudes, skill sets, and knowledge to accomplish its most ambitious Goals.

The following page shows a sample start-up LogFrame that includes typical start-up Outcomes. Don't accept it as is; adjust and adapt it to your project. Are there better ways to express your start-up Goal and Purpose? Review the Outcomes list. What other requirements does your project need? How about additional types of analyses, such as benefits/costs or rate of returns? Assumptions are not shown in this example, but your team should definitely include them in your start-up LogFrame as well.

Use this generic template to jump-start the process of building your team and your project plans together. You'll be delighted at the time it saves getting a smooth and effective start.

Generic Start-Up LogFrame

Objectives	Measures
Goal: Successful Project	1. Project meets identified objectives on-time and within budget. 2. Team enjoys the experience: learns, grows, and feels satisfied. 3. All key stakeholders are pleased.
Purpose: Team gets smooth, quick start.	Within _____ days of formation, team develops and agrees on approach in Start-up LogFrame, accepts their task responsibilities, and is active in implementing.
Outcomes: 1. Project Team formed and functioning	1.1 Key team members identified and recruited by (date)____. 1.2 Team formed and holds initial meeting by _____. 1.3 Team modifies and develops this or similar Pre-Project LogFrame by _____.
2. Stakeholder analysis completed	2.1 Key players and their interests identified by _____, 2.2 Decisions made about who to include in developing the project LogFrame and how to involve other stakeholders.
3. Initial project LogFrame developed	3.1 By _____, team constructs first cut LogFrame for the project. 3.2 LogFrame includes Objectives, Measures, Assumptions, and Tasks, and meets quality standards for a good LogFrame (see checklist in Appendix).
4. Supporting tools and processes developed	4. Team creates WBS, Gantt charts, and/or Responsibility Charts as needed by _____.
5. Execution and monitoring system in place	5. Team decides on how they will monitor progress, report to others, adjust plans, etc.
6. (Other Outcomes as Needed)	

Key Points Review

1. Powerful team-building occurs when teams use the LogFrame. The LogFrame process guides the conversation in a way that efficiently surfaces issues and helps create agreement (or, equally useful, quickly pinpoints areas of disagreement).

2. Size up your stakeholders, their interests, and the degree of support predicated and required. If there is a gap, you have work to do. Become a master student of human moves.

3. The *process* of planning is more crucial than the planning documents which pop out at the other end. The process described here helps you simultaneously build and shape a strong team while they work together to create an actionable plan.

4. Riding the project rollercoaster without getting queasy requires sharpening your Emotional Intelligence. Learn to use your emotions – and that of others – as a powerful and productive project resource.

5. Developing a start-up LogFrame helps the team avoid tunnel vision, sharpen success factors, and get moving swiftly.

Chapter 9: Managing the Strategic Action Cycle

"You have to be fast on your feet or else a strategy is useless"

– Lou Gerstner, IBM

Taking A "Cycle- Logical" Approach

All living organisms have the ability to learn from, and adapt to, their environment. Projects are living systems as well, a collection of human energies, human resources, and human commitment, each focused on defined Objectives. With the exception of "blueprint projects," where every step can be scripted in advance, most project plans will evolve as conditions change, but only if we are "cycle-logical."

Taking a "cycle-logical" approach requires deliberately managing the *strategic action cycle*, the ongoing loop of planning, implementation, and evaluation, followed by re-planning, implementation, and evaluation – repeating the cycle until success is reached (as defined by project Purpose).

Here's the strategic action cycle in visual form:

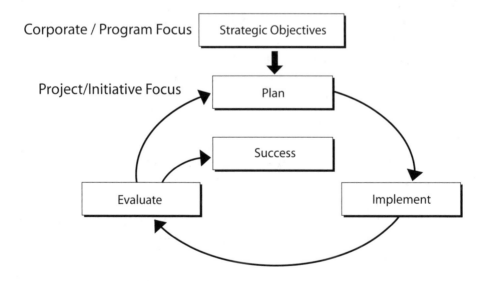

As your project spirals through time in phased cycles of planning, implementation, and evaluation, keep tuned to what project success means, as pre-defined by Objectives and associated Measures. As your project unfolds, you naturally become wiser, but does your project strategy get formally updated in a way that builds on lessons learned? Do the insights and ideas of different team members get factored back in to make your project approach better? Do you have a process to fine-tune the original hypothesis over time?

Being cycle-logical means adjusting efforts that do not appear to be producing the desired results, and celebrating the efforts that are. Being cycle-logical is an ongoing effort that should be committed to in advance, and reinforced throughout the life of the project. Cycle management builds an adaptive mindset into the project by allowing systematic responses to obstacles and opportunities that the project encounters *after* it starts and is underway.

Straight and Curved Path

Let's distinguish between straight line blueprint projects and curved path or emergent projects. With straight-line projects, you can plot a clear path to the end when you start, and manage, more or less, according to plan. When painting a house, for example, after you choose the colors, you buy the paint, and brush, spray, or roll it on. The unknowns are reasonably few and bounded (i.e., will my helpers show up?), and minor changes in the price of paint pigment in Peru won't affect your plans to paint your preferred shade of pale pink.

But in curved path projects, you can only see a limited distance ahead. Think of traversing a mountain road with lots of curves and switch backs. You know the destination and general direction is northwest, but you can't see around the corners. You must round the bend and see the lay of the land before you scope out the next phase of the journey. These emergent projects require dynamic planning with multiple planning iterations as the project moves forward through a continuing cycle of learning.

In curved path projects, it's wise to structure your project into several phases, each of which contributes to an over-arching goal which stays constant, more or less. You plan the first cycle, implement, and then, based on evaluation results, plan the next phase. Cycle-logical planning is always future-focused on upcoming phases, chunks, or cycles. The more mid-course corrections, the better.

Name Your Chunks!

Big doable projects are like uneaten whales: they *can* be eaten, but only one bite at a time. After you are clear about your Purpose and Goal, how do you slice and dice the whole into workable parts and phases? Begin multi-phase projects by identifying phase chunks. Each time you complete a phase or chunk, you need to complete the strategic action cycle by evaluating your degree of success. Each time you evaluate, it's time for a new/revised LogFrame, with probable re-chunking of the Outcomes.

The key to managing the project strategy cycle is found in the chunking concept expressed in the Bizarro cartoon in Chapter Four. You must initially break your effort into logical chunks, usually by named phase, with secondary breakdowns as needed by function, discipline, departments, people involved, time periods, cost accounts, etc. Typical first-order chunking logic is by phases, but other chunking logic occurs *within* each phase. Consider and use whatever chunking criteria makes sense, given your higher objectives. Be cognizant of the rationale behind chunking choices, as well as their implications. Realize that your criteria may shift over time.

For mainstream projects that follow a predictable methodology and life cycle (e.g., product development), standard phase names and gates usually exist (e.g., Design, Build, Test, Operate, Maintain). For non-routine projects, pre-defined phase names do not exist, so you need to characterize and name each phase. For example, the sealed-source project team, named an early phase "Analyze Alternatives" and organized around doing extensive paper studies concerning the characteristics of 15 potential sites).

Strategic chunking is more essential than you might think. I've seen teams stay stuck and stagnate because they failed to chunk their project into meaningful phases and name each phase. Naming phases at the project's start avoids getting into a vague drift which lacks focus, eats energy, saps morale and increases the cost of solution. Chunk smart!

When you face slippery or tricky issues that are difficult to wrap your arms around, call phase one "Problem Definition" and develop a LogFrame. Your phase one LogFrame Purpose might read "problem sufficiently well understood to permit a path forward," and the Outcomes would include tasks such as consulting with stakeholders, conducting analyses, etc.

Monitoring vs. Evaluation

Monitoring and evaluation are both vital, but very different management functions. Monitoring is an ongoing process of keeping track during the shoulder-to-the-wheel driving of the project plan. It accepts the Logical Framework as a "best design" and works to translate Input activities and resources into Outcomes per the plan.

Monitoring	Evaluation
• Constant and ongoing	• Periodic and infrequent
• Focus on Inputs and Outcomes	• Focus on Purpose and Goal
• Accepts design as given	• Challenges design

Evaluation, by contrast, is a periodic but infrequent process that challenges the very design, and calls for a careful review of the strategic hypotheses, especially the Outcome-to-Purpose mix. Evaluation requires you to step back from the day-to-day work and ask different questions, refresh key Assumptions, and refine hypotheses.

For example, monitoring is about patient temperatures, taken hourly, and recorded. Evaluation means asking what the three consecutive readings over 101°F indicate, and asking if we need to *alter our strategy* in light of them?

Obviously, not everything about the project needs to be constantly re-planned, unless you're in an exceptionally fluid situation. The sealed-source recovery team, even after many mid-course corrections, remained clear to its Purpose and Goal: implement an action plan that reduced risk and contributed to human health and safety. Your own Goal will remain reasonably constant, but the Purpose may shift over time, as might the original mix of Outcomes. Changes in the status of Assumptions always introduce issues to react and respond to throughout the project as well.

How to Get Valid Status Information

Monitoring means the ability to put together a reasonable picture of what's happening by actively communicating with task managers, reading reports, juggling email, touching base with key stakeholders, keeping people informed, and whatever else it takes. The dynamics of most projects require that you use multiple means of monitoring to get an informed picture.

Remember that the purpose of your project Management Information System (MIS) is to get the right information to the right people, in the right format, at the right time. Don't fall into the trap of relying only on reports and other system-generated information to monitor status. An effective project MIS not only includes databases, computers, and formal status reports, but also embraces the informal/people processes.

Formal systems provide an incomplete picture, because they miss the "soft stuff," such as whether project team relationships are grounded in trust and open communications. A brief and candid hallway conversation can yield richer information than may be reported in project meetings. Thus, the importance of shaping effective norms, as described in Chapter Eight.

Designing your communication system requires a thoughtful consideration of the nature of information that project team members, executives, and other stakeholders will need. Consider the following thought-jogging questions:

- Who needs to know what information, and for what Purpose?
- What is mission-critical data or information?
- How will critical data be acquired and processed?
- What is "must-have" versus "nice to have" information? What is the benefit/cost of additional data?
- What information will automatically be provided to the organization by existing systems, and what must be "home-grown?"
- Who will have the responsibility for collecting critical data/info?
- How do you set up an effective archiving and retrieval system?

Recognize the importance of the third column of the Logical Framework, Verification. Properly fleshed out, Verifications identify how to get and use necessary information. In addition to monitoring progress toward milestones, make sure to take the pulse of key process indicators, such as the effectiveness of the project team, productivity of meetings, etc. Project reviews shouldn't focus only on progress toward Outcomes, but also on how well the *core-team processes* are working.

Don't Ask This Question

We've all been disappointed or angry when people don't deliver on-time as promised. Reduce these nasty surprises by asking better questions ahead of time so that you know where things stand. The typical (and worst) question project managers ask team members, in order to track status is, *"How's it going on this task?"* Bad question, because you are likely to get misleading responses like "okay" that may mask difficulties. "Tell me where we are on this item" is a much better question that generates dialogue and encourages candor. Here are a few other quality questions to ask:

- Are you having any difficulties that would keep you from meeting targets?
- Are you getting the support you need from others?
- Is there anything else I should know about this?
- What do you need from me?

Making Evaluation Valuable

It's healthy to periodically step back from the day-to-day focus and evaluate where things are. *Schmidt Happens* during every project. New realities pop up. They may be walls, trenches, fire-fights, market shifts, or higher taxes, and these new realities cannot be ignored with a blind, mechanical focus on "our original plan." You must continually ask this ongoing meta-question: *What are we learning and is our strategy working?*

Evaluation is an underused and underappreciated project function. Consider the benefits of these two types of evaluation: formative and summative. Formative evaluation can be a potential mid-stream tool for redirecting and improving a particular project. Summative (also called ex post facto) evaluation can yield lessons learned for use in future projects.

The LogFrame as an Evaluation Guide

Use the LogFrame to stay focused on the intended Objectives by asking questions such as:

- Is our Purpose still valid?

- What's our progress toward Purpose?

- Will this Purpose get us to the Goal?

- What is the status of Assumptions?

- Will our Purpose be achieved?

- Are these the right Outcomes?

- Are we achieving them effectively?

- Which new ones should be added?

- What do we do next?

- What changes will produce better results?

- How should we revise our strategic hypothesis (Outcome to Purpose to Goal) and re-plan?

Changes in the status of a key Assumption can sabotage your project as well as open new options. When the sealed-source project began, it was believed impossible to bury radioactive waste in the Waste Isolation Pilot Project (WIPP), a suitable New Mexico site that was used only for military waste, not civilian waste. So, the task force had originally undertaken extensive studies of fifteen other potential sites. But 9/11 changed everything. The post 9/11 environment eliminated the bureaucratic obstacles to burying the waste in the WIPP. Suddenly, the Outcomes of completed site characterizations were not needed and the in-process task could be dropped.

Remember that evaluation is, itself, a project that takes time and resources. Before committing to evaluation, ask these questions:

- Who cares? Without a clear evaluation user, willing to act on the results, there is little value in proceeding.

- What's the intent? Will this be an evaluation or an inquisition? (Avoid secondary agendas like "nailing" a person).

- What specific questions should the evaluation answer?

- Who should do the evaluation? Insiders? Outside experts? Both?

- What's the plan? How will we identify/collect/analyze data, then organize/synthesize the information, and finally present conclusions and recommendations?

The evaluation scope can be broad or can zoom in on selected areas such as project management methods, soundness of hypotheses, impact on Purpose and Goal, team effectiveness, resource utilization, and secondary effects. For instance, market dynamics may be blowing the schooner of corporate sales across a lake of opportunity, but evaluation may reveal that you'll soon be off-course unless you tack slightly back toward your Goal.

Evaluation Data and Methods

Another great advantage of using the LogFrame is that while designing the project, you also establish the basis for later evaluation. Your Purpose, Measures and Verifications give a solid head start to evaluation.

The Fircrest School project, previously discussed (see the full LogFrame in the Appendix), provides an outstanding example of how to identify data needed for evaluation at the time of project design. The Purpose Measures spelled out in advance the necessary data, while the Verification column showed how it should be gathered. Together, Measures and Verifications should identify what data you might need to collect on a regular basis from day one, or at least establish a baseline to work from.

It is reasonable to expect that some project teams will not know exactly what data is needed to verify progress at the beginning of their project. In this case, explicitly create an Outcome devoted to learning what is required, so that evaluative data can, and will, be collected in an ongoing and timely manner. It's likely that some of the means identified in the Verification column may not currently exist and need to be created under an Outcome called "Develop Verification Systems." This is another example of how information in one cell of the matrix can impact other cells.

Periodic evaluation can yield project-saving decisions, but only if the relevant data exists. It's frustrating to find that the necessary evaluation data, which could and should have been collected on an ongoing basis, is not available to help make informed decisions.

An ex post evaluation occurs after project completion. Invest the time to glean kernels of wisdom from the project so that future efforts will have the benefit of lessons learned with 20-20 hindsight. An ex post evaluation might examine these important questions:

- To what extent were Outcomes produced and Purpose achieved?

- What was the impact on Goal?

- What went right, and why?

- What went wrong? Were we to do this over again, what would we do differently?

- What were the secondary effects of the rights *and* the wrongs?

- What Assumptions may have been invalid?

- What did we learn that was worth learning?

- How can insights and learning be shared and integrated organization-wide?

- How do we codify our learning and apply the lessons to future efforts (pamphlets, case studies, knowledge banks, web-pages, etc.)?

After the project is done there will be all kinds of reasons *not* to evaluate, i.e., people are too weary, too drained, or moving on to other things. Guard against this by building an evaluation milestone into the project plan, so it is there from the beginning and the expectations are clear.

On occasion, you'll encounter unplanned events that attach a cachet of negativity to the project. You reached your Goals, but just as everything was about to come to an unmitigated success, one of your delivery trucks ran over Narfy the Dog, casting a pall of angst over those in your organization who were fond of old Narfy. Step up and defuse these unfortunate finale-killers, as quickly as possible.

Don't treat setbacks or embarrassments as something beneath the dignity of your organization to deal with effectively. The accidents which happen along the way need smoothing over, so smooth whatever the hiccup is, quickly, humanely, and compassionately.

During the Tylenol scare, when saboteurs laced on-the-shelf bottles with poison, Johnson and Johnson rapidly responded without attempting a coverup. They were widely praised for reassuring the public, and their stock price rose because they handled it well.

Success vs. Completion

Project completion and project success are two different concepts. When Outcomes have been delivered, your project may be done, but it is not really successful until Purpose has been reached. Sometimes Purpose occurs without all of the sealed sources being delivered due to external influences on the project, as with the OSRP project. The ability to place these sealed-source wastes in an already established facility eliminated the need for extensive studies on 15 other potential sites. So, the project was a success, even though most of the initially planned tasks were not completed.

Celebrating Success

My philosophy is simple: celebrate success early and often. Every worthwhile project has pushed people through frustration, disappointments and setbacks. But with commitment and spunk, good people rise to new heights of accomplishment. Along the way, simple recognition, like bringing a big box of bagels to project meetings, leaves a good taste in people's mouths. When the end arrives, recognize and reward participants. Team efforts should be heralded openly, publicly, and joyfully. Can you create a ceremony or ritual that signals and celebrates the end?

More elaborate rewards, such as promotions, study sabbaticals, vacations, cash bonuses, or awards presentations, may also be appropriate at the project celebration. Make it worth the candle for all participants, but in particular for anyone who might be perceived as "the little guy," so that your organization is seen as fair and just in rewarding effort, particularly on-target effort that benefits the whole organization. Make it special enough to be interesting. Let spouses come, or invite some organization Big Shots. Go beyond mere mechanics and make yours a *Project-Ender to Remember!*

Key Points Review

1. Monitoring and evaluation are linked processes with very different functions. Monitoring asks "are we on track?" while evaluation asks, "are we on the *right* track?"

   Manage successive iterations of the Plan-Implement-Evaluate cycle. While monitoring verifies that we're actively moving, only evaluation can assure us that we're moving to *toward our Purpose and Goal.*

2. Monitoring is an ongoing process of watching progress towards Outcomes. Evaluation is an infrequent, occasional process that examines impact and linkages at the Purpose and Goal levels. Do both.

3. To stay sufficiently nimble over time, build in evaluation and re-planning events. Make sure your "original plan" includes its own self-adapting mechanisms, which are a sign of life in living organisms. This can be accomplished simply by scheduling major project evaluations as milestones.

4. Remember to acknowledge forward progress and celebrate small victories along the path to project success.

Chapter 10: Applying These Ideas In Your World

"Man with open mouth must wait long time for roast duck to fly in."

– Chinese proverb

Exploring a Dozen Dynamic Directions

You have seen that the LogFrame offers a versatile strategic thinking process. Now, what will you do with these concepts and tools? It's really up to you. Begin with the issues currently on your plate. Scan your internal environment; look for "hot-button" topics and start there. Be opportunistic.

The potential applications are virtually limitless. Ken Howell, a Sony Electronics champion of this method says "show me something that this *doesn't* apply to." Ken points out that every major or minor project rests on a strategic hypothesis involving multiple Objectives, Measures, and Assumptions. The LogFrame integrates those core requirements with elegant simplicity while protecting against erroneous thinking. Apply it bountifully!

If you read this book with a specific current or upcoming project in mind, your head may already be whirling with possible Objectives, Measures, and Assumptions. That's great! Get your team together, follow the application steps at the ends of Chapters 4-7, and you'll end up with a valuable product.

You can take the LogFrame in many different directions. Here are one dozen high-payoff ways that my clients in government, private companies, and research organizations have applied these methods. More possibilities may emerge for you as you read about how others have used this tool. The Appendix includes brief client case-studies and their project LogFrames for the first six of these dynamic applications.

1. **Develop or Update the Strategic Plan**. This thinking method supports a broader strategic planning process that is critical to any organization. Regardless of the context in which you operate, at least annually it is wise to review and redefine your portfolio of strategic projects. Prioritize them and create LogFrame plans for the most essential ones.

The case-study in the Appendix shows how the Safety and Security Division of Lawrence Livermore National Laboratory did just that. This example also illustrates how an outside process consultant can catalyze an organization's strategic planning.

2. **Strengthen Teams Across Work Functions**. The LogFrame helps bring together a new, diverse, or cross-functional team. The four simple questions and logical matrix provide a common vocabulary and structure to work smoothly across organizational boundaries. This case study shows how ARINC, an Annapolis systems engineering company, used this tool to unite executive level task forces.

3. **Reinvent Your Department.** From time to time, take a fresh look at where you are and where you need to go, and then develop strategies to get there. When performance levels are less than required, or your mission changes, this becomes a necessity. In the case study, the Facilities Maintenance Unit at the Los Alamos National Laboratory aimed at nothing less than a total transformation to meet growing customer demands.

4. **Develop Information Technology Solutions and Algorithms.** The LogFrame offers a general-purpose analytic tool that helps structure algorithms of every sort, and integrates technology solutions into core processes. Our case study example, from the U.S. Department of Energy, illustrates the design of an anomaly tracking system supporting the annual certification of nuclear stockpile reliability.

5. **Design and Launch Marketing or Sales Initiatives.** Flesh out initiatives that support strategic sales goals or balanced scorecard elements. This case study describes how an Asian international joint venture company planned to expand sales of a cancer-treating medical supplement in the provincial areas of Thailand.

6. **Close Out Projects With a People Focus**. Bringing a major project to an end requires not only wrapping up the documentation, but helping team members transition to new situations. Forward-thinking leaders at the Washington State Department of Transportation organized this close-out for a major bridge project in a way that met all federal and state contract requirements and helped all project staff find new positions.

7. **Develop Recommendations and Make Decisions**. Use this tool to be systematic and transparent about how to set decision criteria, identify alternatives, collect information, conduct analyses, and make recommendations.

8. **Improve Critical Processes.** Identify and harvest the "low-hanging fruit," where a modest process improvement effort yields big returns. The LogFrame can be used to analyze and redesign any process that needs an overhaul.

9. **Handle Emergent Issues.** Got a hot potato? This approach works well on non-standard projects that arise suddenly and need clear solution roadmaps. Slice, dice, and serve up your project potato by defining your problem or issue, converting it into Objectives, and structuring the strategic hypothesis for a smart solution.

10. **Unstick Stuck Stuff.** Take a fresh look at stalled projects, programs, and strategies; identify and evaluate alternatives; and redirect your efforts along promising directions. Use a LogFrame at any project phase to plan and execute current and future phases. Break loose from myopic thinking by brainstorming fresh Purpose statements and see what new possibilities emerge.

11. **Structure Project Evaluations.** The LogFrame can be used to organize evaluations of ongoing projects in the portfolio as well as completed projects. The LogFrame Purpose will help clarify the evaluation focus, and the Outcomes will identify the various analytic and information chunks you need to make informed decisions.

12. **Organize Learning and Development.** This tool works well to sharpen learning and development programs at all levels. Purpose describes desired behavior change; Goal highlights the expected benefits; Outcomes define the learning delivery system. Intact teams often use this tool to identify and develop the future competencies needed. What new skills or cross-training does your team need?

Try as I might, whittling the possibilities down to a dozen was difficult. Here are two bonus applications beyond these dynamic dozen.

13. **Take a High Level First Cut.** Planning a research program to find intelligent life on Mars? Purchasing a remote island and starting your own country? Use the LogFrame as a front-end tool for high-level scoping of super-sized projects.

14. **Adjunct for Outside-the-Box Projects**. If your organization has a formal project development system, with phases and gates, this approach can provide a refreshing and practical adjunct. For example, Procter & Gamble has a superb system for bringing new products to market, but their well-tuned new-product-development system is not designed to handle initiatives such as developing excellent teamwork, fostering a culture of excellence, or re-evaluating corporate goals. The LogFrame offer a fresh perspective for just about anything that doesn't fit your organization's standard project management methodology.

Peering Through a Wider Strategic Lens

The LogFrame has multiple uses on a stand-alone basis, as described in this book. But the ability to *Turn Strategy Into Action* presumes that there is a sound, overarching strategy to begin with. However, this is not always true.

We still haven't covered all the possible applications. What ideas come to mind for how *you* might profitably apply this approach?

Motivated leaders at all levels who need a front-end strategic planning model will appreciate the following 5-step process map, which graphically incorporates all of the tools and concepts in this book. In addition, this map includes additional practical tools which offer you a wider angle, far-reaching strategic lens.

This graphic has evolved over many years to show how the LogFrame, and all of the other elements detailed in this book, fit nicely together in an organized management system (Step 3 captures the LogFrame tool). Keep it handy as you begin to use this approach and apply these tools. This map comes from my companion book, *The 5-Step Process Road-Map for Turning Strategy Into Action*, which gives equal attention to all five steps and provides how-to tips for each block in the map. (You'll find a color download of this at *www.ManagementPro.com.*)

The LogFrame should be the cornerstone of any more ambitious, organization-wide strategic planning effort that identifies a set of key strategies, projects, and/or initiatives.

Turning Strategy Into Action

Process Road Map - Planning for Successful Execution

1. Organize: Build A Strong Foundation

1.1 Involve Key Stakeholders

Who does this include, affect or concern?

1.2 Organize the Core Team

Who are the key players needed to get started?

1.3 Choose Common Approach

What process & tools should we use?

1.4 Plan for the Plan

PLAN

What's the best way to start fast and smart?

2. Strategize: Paint the Big Picture

2.1 Clarify the Context

What's the problem, issue and system of interest?

2.2 Examine Environ-mental Factors

Which external and internal factors affect us?

2.3 Clarify Major Objectives

What's the vision, goal and other objectives?

2.4 Chunk and Choose

How should we organize this into logical chunks?

3. Projectize: Develop Logical Framework(s)

3.1 Define and Align Objectives

What are we trying to accomplish and why?

3.2 Develop Success Measures

How will we measure success?

3.3 Surface & Test Assumptions

What other conditions must exist?

3.4 Identify Action Steps

How do we get there? (tasks, budgets & schedules)

4. Harmonize: Make the Team Work

4.1 Determine Project Structure

Where is the project located?

4.2 Set Norms & Guiding Principles

What norms agreements, and principles will we follow?

4.3 Clarify Roles & Responsibilities

What are the roles and responsibilities of key players?

4.4 Apply Emotional Intelligence

How can we manage moods as a project resource?

5. Actionize: Get to the Goal

5.1 Monitor & Communicate

What's s the status of mile-stones & assumptions?

5.2 Manage the Learning Cycle

How do we review, replan, and recommit?

5.3 Evaluate and Improve

Is our strategy working and what are we learning?

5.4 Conclude and Celebrate

How can we conclude and acknowledge the team?

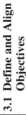

Doing the Project RAP (Rapid Action Planning)

The best way to grow a project strategy in the minds and hearts of key people is through a well-structured "RAP" (Rapid Action Planning) session. In these focused planning workshops, the core team, plus other major stakeholders, flesh out a project strategy using the LogFrame to guide the conversation and document the results. This gets things started on the right track, even if some details are still hazy. RAP events follow custom-designed agendas that fit the project context, and are often professionally facilitated.

How long does this take? It really depends. A small or medium project might take half-a-day to two days to sketch out sufficiently, and even large initiatives can be "80% planned" after two or three days of continuous or intermittent planning. Large projects do not necessarily require longer initial planning time. Core segments can usually be broken off and begun while additional planning proceeds in an ongoing parallel effort.

The quick formula for a successful team RAP session is summarized here, and then explained further below:

1. Key players and core team members attend.

2. Session is facilitated by a process consultant (who is outside the project).

3. A meeting room is set up to foster productive results.

4. Use the LogFrame structure and methodology.

5. Capture key results, record decisions, and document action items.

1. Invite the Key Players

Who are your 3-7 core team members? These are the people you want there. You can also invite your high-level champions for the entire session, or just to kick it off by sharing their expectations at the session start. Alternately, they can join in at the end of the session to review the draft design, offer comments, and learn what is expected of them.

Make sure that everyone on the team has read this book and is familiar with these tools beforehand, or be prepared to spend some time educating them yourself. Having a common framework and planning language will harmonize your team and accelerate your thinking.

2. Bring an Outside Process Facilitator In

The key word in process facilitator is *process*. A skilled facilitator makes all the difference in the world. You know, first-hand, how difficult it is to be a competent project manager. Well, it's even more difficult to be a competent project manger and a good facilitator at the same time. While exceptions exist, people who try to fill both roles usually end up doing both poorly.

For major projects, bring in a neutral, but skilled, facilitator who is outside the "project system" to guide the RAP sessions. This might be an external consultant or an internal facilitator. Seasoned facilitators do not feel threatened if they are required to ask hard questions, point out gaps, or bring a rambling discussion back on track. Their expertise at enabling meetings to move forward productively makes them a smart investment.

Of course, you may not have the option of using an external facilitator, so I've included some guidelines for flying solo later in the chapter.

3. Set up the Room for Productive Results

Meeting room setups dramatically affect the quality of your process and results. Your group will generate a lot of information, which you want to rapidly capture and plug in when and where it's needed.

Consider how to set up the room for maximum interaction and idea capture. Keep information visible to all during the process. The best results occur when everyone can see their ideas being plugged into a large LogFrame grid. For this reason, it's best to work from a large whiteboard or blackboard on which you sketch a LogFrame grid. (See website www.ManagementPro.com for a large, attractive, laminated, reusable LogFrame grid, ideal for team use.) Another option is to link a computer to an LCD projector and display the LogFrame grid as a work in progress.

Have a flip chart pad (or two), plenty of marking pens, and masking tape to paste up pages on the walls. Post key ideas where all can see, add to, and own their ideas.

Having a large LogFrame visible to all supports a collaborative team approach. The least effective way is to write responses on a pad of paper where only one person can see them. Also avoid having one person keep notes of the LogFrame on his personal notebook or computer while everyone else sits around a table. The energy of collaboratively putting the LogFrame together visibly multiplies enthusiasm and builds shared commitment.

4. Follow the LogFrame Structure and Methodology

The four critical strategic questions offer a user-friendly, jargon-free way to get the group started. Go deeper with the detailed trigger questions found in Chapter Four to complete the LogFrame elements. Ask them lots of questions to coax out and fine-tune the project design.

As the discussion proceeds, listen carefully. Without necessarily using the Log Frame terminology, people will describe Objectives, Measures, and Assumptions. Your task is to put their ideas into the LogFrame structure appropriately.

After you have the vertical logic in place (Goal, Purpose, and Outcomes), you may proceed to either Assumptions or Measures. This is iterative work that will benefit from adjustments and refinements as the RAP session proceeds.

5. Capture the Results

At the start, have the team decide how they will record the information they generate. Draft somebody with a laptop to capture and circulate the end results. Better yet, assign one or more people the task of writing up the final results. Having two sets of eyes working on any document ensures greater accuracy and more thorough information capture.

You can also capture flipchart sheets and work products pasted to the wall with a high-resolution digital camera, and transcribe them later.

Facilitating By Yourself

When you play the facilitative role, use these guidelines:

- Focus on defining the big picture first, then the details.

- Understand the key players' interests and concerns.

- Build productive team norms and communication patterns.

- Encourage active but balanced involvement of all participants.

Like an orchestra conductor, you do not play an instrument. Rather, you wield the baton to draw information from the players' heads, help them to harmonize their abilities, and improvise like jazz players to produce satisfying music.

Even when you have more expertise than the group members, do not be overly directive in steering them toward any single approach. Let them own it too. Your role is to build from the ideas of the group, not supply all of the right answers. If you want to make substantive comments, call "time-out" and let the group know you are stepping out of your process facilitation role for a moment to make your subject matter comment, then return to that role.

Experience shows that a good design, developed and supported by the team, has a much better chance of success than a perfect design developed by a project manager (or external consultant) with little team involvement.

Techniques for Guiding Your Team

Questions are your primary tool for steering the group, starting with the four critical questions. Ask lots of questions and work their answers into the LogFrame cells. You will often need to read between the lines to interpret and supportively restate their responses before plugging them into the LogFrame.

While the LogFrame provides focus, don't let it limit you. Allow and encourage broader discussion about the environment, project context, and dependencies.

Skilled facilitators often use flip charts to capture raw ideas and move selected information into a LogFrame grid as the discussion makes it apparent where all the information fits. This technique allows you to incorporate all of the good ideas while ignoring those that do not fit.

Team comments will often reveal a clear project approach, but you may need to sharpen their thinking:

- Suggest different phraseology. For example, you may say, "By 'make it work better,' do you mean 'improve system operations?'"

- Point out and test project linkages. You can increase shared understanding by showing how things fit together using LogFrame logic.

- Integrate comments made by various members. For example, "John said the project Objective is to deploy the new product, and Bill said the Objective is to increase market share. Does it make sense that, if you deploy the new product, you will increase sales, which will increase market share?"

Now It's Up to You

Congratulations on completing this book! There is much meaty material here, so keep the book handy, reread it often, make notes in the margins, and customize your approach as you apply the ideas.

By now, you can appreciate that this up-front investment of time and energy in planning pays handsome dividends in avoiding problems, saving time, and reaching project goals faster. But, when all is said and done, the greatest benefit of the Logical Framework approach is not in knowing about it, but in *using it*.

I have stressed that using the LogFrame is a process, and that the process is more important than the resulting project plan. The ultimate value from using the LogFrame is to change how you and others think. This tool combines project planning with team building (which is important), but its best contribution is really in getting people to think deeply about how to make their project succeed in a fast-paced, highly competitive environment.

The final product is almost irrelevant if people master the art of thinking strategically, because that yields the greatest long-term benefit. The LogFrame plan merely documents your thinking processes and demonstrates that the process has been rigorous. Your completed LogFrame offers a *Means of Verification* that shows you've embraced the right questions, and that a quality planning process has occurred. At the end, all should truly understand *why* they are doing the project, as well as the *how, who, what, and when.*

The next best benefit of the Logical Framework is in *having it completed* and shared, so that all involved in executing it can do so in a timely, harmonized manner. Having a brief document, in the LogFrame format, in the hands of all key stakeholders and executive team members, keeps everyone on-path and focused.

I strongly encourage you to commit to doing at least one LogFrame within the next week. Research shows that retention of learning new skills increases dramatically when practiced soon after initial exposure. You'll maximize the payoff from your investment in reading this book by applying the information quickly, while it is still fresh in your mind.

Keep it simple. Don't get hung up on how to fill in all of the blanks. Review it with the self-scoring checklist in the Appendix, but avoid trying to make it great or "perfect" – just get the first version done. Then make it better.

My best wishes for your project and professional success. I'd love to hear about how you are using this planning and action system to gain the strategic edge in your work and life. Reading about your success makes my day!

Appendix Table of Contents

Logical Framework

for _____(Project name)

Prepared by:_____   Date Prepared_____   © 2007 Terry Schmidt   www.managementpro.com   Used by permission

OBJECTIVES Logical hierarchy of if-then objectives	SUCCESS MEASURES Conditions which indicate that objectives have been achieved	VERIFICATION Source of evidence to verify Measures	ASSUMPTIONS Additional factors necessary for success
GOAL:	GOAL MEASURES:		Assumptions to reach goal
PURPOSE:	PURPOSE MEASURES:		Assumptions to achieve Purpose
OUTCOMES:	OUTCOME MEASURES:		Assumptions to achieve Outcomes

INPUTS: Activities & Resources			Schedule (in weeks, months, etc.)	Assumptions for activities
Activities	Responsibility	Resources		
1. Outcome #1				
1.1				
1.2				
1.3				
2. Outcome #2				
2.1				
2.2				
2.3				
3. Outcome #3				
3.1				
3.2				
3.3				
4. Outcome #4				
4.1				
4.2				
4.3				
5. Outcome #5				
5.1				
5.2				
5.3				
6. Outcome #6				
6.1				
6.2				
6.3				

Glossary of Terms

Activities   The action steps or tasks to be undertaken, and resources necessary to produce Outcomes.

Assumptions   External factors that influence the success or failure over which the project manager lacks direct control. Assumptions can be monitored, influenced, and sometimes managed.

Baseline Data   Data describing the conditions when a project is started. Provides a basis to assess the nature and extent of change caused by the project.

Bottom-Up   In LogFrame terms, beginning at the Input level and using *if-then* thinking to link to Outcomes, Purpose and Goal. Bottom-up thinking can test the causal logic of a strategy and validate top-down planning.

Chunking   The logical grouping of information into "chunks" according to appropriate and functional criteria.

Chunking Logic   Criteria chosen for organizing the project; includes phase, function, discipline, etc. Be clear about your logic.

Coupling   Situations in which one element of a project affects or depends upon the implementation of an element from another project. Coupling (or dependencies) can be acknowledged by making Assumptions in the LogFrames.

Decision Tree   A graphic tool for portraying a hierarchy of independent conditions, choices, events and the Outcomes resulting from each valid combination of conditions.

Disaggregation   Breaking down a large or complex Objective into smaller components – chunking down.

End-Of-Project   The set of success Measures that signals achievement of the project Purpose and thus, the success of the project. Identify and gain agreement on these Measures in advance.

Evaluation Status (EOPS)   An orderly examination of progress at each level of Objective. Examines the validity of hypotheses, challenges project approach, and identifies redesign and replanning actions. Evaluation reviews Outcome-Purpose and Purpose-Goal linkages, while monitoring focuses on the Input-Outcome linkage.

Execution   The process and systems for moving plans into action and achieving project objectives.

Flow Diagram   A graphic tool depicting the operation of a system as a network of activities. Shows origins, directions and sequences of decisions and events.

Gantt Chart   Also called a bar chart, this graphic tool helps schedule and monitor project tasks and activities. Gantt charts display key activities vertically, and estimate activity duration against a horizontal time scale.

Goal   The higher level, broader strategic, or program Objective immediately above project Purpose. Goal specifies the "*then*" statement for which the project Purpose (plus Purpose-level assumptions) provides a plausible "*if*".

Horizontal Logic   A term which expresses the combination of Objectives, Success Measures and Means of Verification at each level.

Hypothesis	An educated guess; a predictive statement about a causal relationship involving uncertainty. The predicted and intended means-end relationship between each level in the Logical Framework constitutes a set of linked, *if-then* hypotheses.
If-Then Thinking	The basic premise of cause-effect, means-ends thinking.
Indicator	Indicators are part of success Measures. Indicators are targeted by a description of quantity, quality (performance), and time, as well as by cost and client/customer.
Inputs	Activities and the resources (time, money, people) needed to produce each Outcome.
Leading Indicators	Success Measures that are observable now, which also predict the future status of Objectives.
Linked Hypotheses	A series of predictive *if-then* statements about project relationships which show up in the Objectives column of the LogFrame.
Logical Framework	A set of interlocking concepts organized into a 4x4 matrix, which helps to logically design sound projects.
Logical Clusters	A bundle of activities and Outcomes based on a real or imagined similarity of implementation. Cluster themes can be drawn from across different projects, programs, or organizational elements to provide synergy, operating economies, or other implementation benefits.
Management Contract	An agreement that the Project Manager will deliver Outcomes given the required Inputs (and valid Assumptions), aimed at achieving Purpose.

Manageable Interest   Defines the responsibility of the Project Manager, which is to deliver Outcomes that will achieve Purpose aimed at achieving the agreed upon Goal. The project manager commits, and is held accountable, to produce Outcomes by effectively managing the activities, given appropriate levels of resources. It is within his/her "Manageable Interest" to modify activities, and do whatever else is necessary to produce Outcomes.

Master Activity List   Thorough list of all the key activities required to produce project Outcomes. A basis for creating core management tools – resource budget, schedules, and agreement charts.

Matrix for the Logical Framework   A 4x4 matrix that displays the interrelationships of the design and evaluation components of a project. The matrix is divided into four rows (for Goal, Purpose, Outcomes, and Inputs), and four columns (for Objectives, Success Measures, Verification, and Assumptions).

Means of Verification   The source and means of obtaining data which will be used to verify an indicator or Measure (e.g., market share as determined by the Marketing Department.)

Monitoring   The management function of following the progress and overseeing the operations of a project. Monitoring focuses on the Input-to-Outcome linkage of the Logical Framework, in contrast to evaluation, which focuses on Outcome-to-Purpose and Purpose-to-Goal linkages.

Network   A graphic representation of the logical sequence of activities and events required to reach a specified Objective.

Objective   A desired project result or intention. Can be an Outcome, Purpose, Goal, or Super Goal.

Objectives Tree   A visual array of Objectives arranged in cause-effect hierarchies.

Outcomes   The specifically intended results believed necessary and sufficient to achieve Purpose. Outcomes can be expected to result from good management of Input activities. "Management contracts" center around responsibility for Outcome production.

Playthroughs   The mental execution of project implementation by the project team using what-if scenarios to identify weaknesses, spot potential problems, and design around them. (In systems design, this is often called a dynamic design review, or run through.)

Program   A "project" consisting of groups of projects all contributing to the same Goal. A program is managed to achieve a Goal, just as a project is managed to achieve a Purpose.

Project   Classic definition: An organized system of interrelated activities and processes established to achieve Objectives within a specified time. Schmidt definition: Engines of Change.

Project Cycle   A systems perspective of a project which considers the three distinct phases of a project (design, implementation, and evaluation) as an integrated system.

Project Design   A summary of what the project is expected to achieve (Goal and Purpose), what it must deliver to achieve Purpose (Outcomes), and how it will deliver Outcomes (Inputs). The key elements of a project design may be summarized in the Logical Framework format.

Project Implementation Management System (PIMS)

A set of interrelated management tools and techniques for use in each phase of the project cycle that are based on a common set of management principles and a common language.

Project Manager

The individual who holds him/herself personally accountable for the success of a project. More specifically, the individual responsible for producing the agreed-upon Outcomes with given Inputs within the specified time and cost constraints.

Purpose

What is hoped to be achieved by undertaking the project; the real motivation. Purpose describes the anticipated change in behavior or system conditions expected when the required Outcomes are produced.

RAP (Rapid Action Planning) Session

Focused workshops to build key products with a core team quickly, while establishing good team norms.

Reporting

Providing relevant project information to appropriate people for timely decision-making. Includes both formal and informal communications, such as reports, meeting notes or personal discussions).

Scientific Method

Procedures for pursuing knowledge through formulating a hypothesis and testing its validity through experimentation.

Strategy

An organized set of programs and projects implemented in order to achieve the organization's vision.

Success Measures   Measures that have quantity, quality, and
                              time targets. Stated in terms such that, an
                              informed skeptic and a proponent of the
                              project would agree on what progress has or
                              has not been made. Measures should be estab-
                              lished during the design phase of a project to
                              provide the basis for subsequent monitoring
                              and evaluation.

SWAG   Acronym for the term "Scientifically Wild
                              Assed Guess," an approach for targeting
                              Measures when there is very little history or
                              prior experience. Considered more scientific
                              than a simple WAG. Not to be confused with
                              the less accurate guestimating technique
                              known as PFA (Plucked From Air)

System   A set of interrelated elements which work
                              together to reach the overall Objectives.
                              Systems are generally described as a
                              strategy or throughput process for producing
                              Outcomes from given Inputs. Key aspects of
                              a system occur in a defined environment.

Top-Down Planning   Proceeding from the general to the particular,
                              or from the broad to the detailed. In the
                              LogFrame, beginning with Goal or Purpose,
                              then proceeding to Outcomes and Inputs.

Tree Analysis   A group of graphic tools used in problem
Structure   diagnosis and Objective setting. This group
                              includes: Problem Trees, Objective Trees,
                              Decision Trees, and Alternative Trees. Tree
                              Analysis is based on the concepts of cause-
                              and-effect relationships and chunking.

Vertical Logic   Represents a prediction that *if* the expected
                                      results at one level of the LogFrame hierarchy
                                      are achieved, and *if* the Assumptions at that
                                      level are valid, *then* the expected results at the
                                      next higher level will be achieved.

Work Breakdown   Tool for disaggregating a system or Objective
Structure   into component parts. Each Outcome is
                                      broken down into smaller components. The
                                      process continues to develop logical work
                                      packages which can be costed, scheduled,
                                      assigned and implemented.

Logical Framework Quality Checklist

Review each element of your LogFrame against these criteria.

Goal Check

___Yes ___No ___?   1.   Supports or describes an important strategic objective.

___Yes ___No ___?   2.   Stated clearly in measurable terms.

___Yes ___No ___?   3.   Not the project name, a restatement, or summary of the Purpose/Outcomes.

Purpose Check

___Yes ___No ___?   4.   LogFrame has a single Purpose, clearly stated.

___Yes ___No ___?   5.   Describes change in behavior, performance or conditions expected.

___Yes ___No ___?   6.   Describes impact expected from Outcomes, doesn't summarize them.

___Yes ___No ___?   7.   A level above the implementation team's direct control.

___Yes ___No ___?   8.   Purpose, plus Assumptions, are both *necessary and sufficient* to reach the Goal.

Outcomes Check

___Yes ___No ___?   9.   Outcomes clearly describe what the team can deliver or make happen.

___Yes ___No ___?   10. The Outcomes are logically chunked. No overlaps/gaps.

___Yes ___No ___?   11. All Outcomes necessary to achieve Purpose are included (none missing).

___Yes ___No ___?   12. Each Outcome is necessary to achieve Purpose (no non essentials).

___Yes ___No ___?   13. Collectively, this set of Outcomes will achieve Purpose.

___Yes ___No ___?   14. Outcomes, plus Assumptions, are both *necessary and sufficient* to achieve Purpose.

Activities Check

___Yes ___No ___?   15. The key activities for each Outcome have been listed.

___Yes ___No ___?   16. Activities are chunked at roughly the same level of detail.

___Yes ___No ___?   17. Together, the activities can produce the Outcomes.

Measures Check

___Yes ___No ___?   18. Specific in terms of quantity, quality, and time.

___Yes ___No ___?   19. Measure what is important about each Objective.

___Yes ___No ___?   20. Each Measure has a practical means of verification

___Yes ___No ___?   21. Changes in status of Measures attributable to achievement of Objective.

Assumptions Check

___Yes ___No ___?   22. Formulated as desirable, positive conditions that must exist for valid *if-then* logic.

___Yes ___No ___?   23. Placed at the level of Objective they affect.

___Yes ___No ___?   24. Clearly stated and include Measures as appropriate.

___Yes ___No ___?   25. Cover all key outside factors that impact the project.

General Check

___Yes ___No ___?   26. Acronyms and abbreviations have been spelled out.

___Yes ___No ___?   27. The logic among Inputs, Outcomes, Purpose and Goal is realistic as a whole.

___Yes ___No ___?   28. Developed by, or will be reviewed by, key players.

___Yes ___No ___?   29. Permits development of linked tools (WBS, Gannt, etc.).

Logical Framework Application Case Studies

The following case studies illustrate a variety of client applications of the LogFrame. These cases are all excerpted from the *Strategic Project Management Solutions Handbook*, a compilation of 53 different client LogFrames. Many of these serve as basic templates that you can modify and use to fit your projects.

Organization Turnaround and Best Practice Example
(Fircrest School for the Developmentally Disabled)

Fircrest School for the Developmentally Disabled is a residential home for some 800 adults and children who suffer from serious mental, physical and emotional developmental disabilities. Fircrest is funded both by Washington State and federal funds, and is managed by the Washington State Department of Social and Health Services.

Several disturbing incidents indicated that residents were not being properly treated, and their quality of life was low. There were some unexplained injuries to residents, and even one suspicious death. Visiting experts noted an overuse of psychoactive medications and restraints. Quality assurance was lacking. Medical and nursing care records were not timely and accurate. Too many nurses were assigned to administrative duties and too few to resident care and treatments.

Following an audit, federal certification was revoked, along with millions of dollars of federal funding. This presented Fircrest management with a serious problem that needed solving quickly, and in the right way. Katie Cameron was tasked with correcting this situation by improving the safety, health, quality of care, and human rights of the residents. Cameron used the Logical Framework with her project team to develop a strategy to regain federal certification.

This example reflects a best practice use of Strategic Thinking and project design using LogFrame concepts. In particular, it includes good Measures and Verifications at all levels, along with a clear and well-organized work plan (Input level).

Review this project design using the LogFrame quality checklist in the Appendix and you'll see it scores *yes* on all of the criteria.

Logical Framework for
Improving Social Service Delivery (Fircrest School for the Developmentally Disabled)

O JECTIVES	MEASURES	HOW TO VERIFY	ASSUMPTIONS
oal: Federal certification standards are achieved and maintained at Fircrest School.	1. Sometime after October 31, all ICF/MR regulatory surveys will be completed with no findings of conditional level deficiencies. 2. Fircrest continues to operate at high standards of health, safety, quality care & human rights.	1. Written decision from survey team with no conditional level findings 2. Follow up annual surveys with no negative findings.	*Assumptions to reach goal* 1. DSHS Secretary does not make agreement with government that Hillcrest is unaware of. 2. No unanticipated Federal government (HCFA or Dept. of Justice) litigation actions. 3. State Attorney General will have plan in place to file appeal by 8/3.
Purpose: People who live at Fircrest are safe, healthy, receive quality care and their human rights are protected.	1. A 50% reduction in resident injury that requires nursing or medical care or intervention occurs between 1/1 and 10/31. 2. No unusual or suspicious resident deaths occur between 1/1 and 10/31. 3. An 80% reduction in restraints and time out use will be achieved between 1/1 and 10/31. 4. A 25% reduction in number of residents beings prescribed psychoactive medication occurs between 1/1 and 10/31. 5. 75% of residents are engaged in paid work activities for three or more hours per day by 9/1.	1.1 Review and summarize incident reports 1.2 Review/tabulate injuries from medical notes 2. Review coroner reports 3. Review & summarize restraint & time out records. 4. Review pharmacy/drug administration records. 5. Collect, review & summarize resident production records & paycheck information.	*Assumptions to reach purpose:* 1. Resident injuries are all reported on incident reports and progress notes. 2. Coroner conducts autopsies on all deaths. 3. Staff fill out restraint/time out records. 4. Production records are kept with sufficient detail.

O JECTIVES		MEASURES		HOW TO VERIFY		ASSUMPTIONS
OUTCOMES:						*Assumptions to produce outcomes:*
1. New resident habilitation program system is implemented.	1.1	By July 1, 95% of resident (awake) hours will be organized and managed by new treatment programs.	1.	Observe each hour of program at each training site.	1.	Staff are adequately trained and aware of new program expectations.
2. Quality Assurance system is implemented to maintain habilitation program changes.	2.1	At least 10 FTEs are assigned to conduct QA activities.	2.1	Check personnel records.	2.	Union agreement can be reached.
	2.2	QA checklist with target program indicators is implemented in all training locations.	2.2	Checklist published.		
	2.3	QA data is used by program teams to modify/ revise/ correct faulty programs.	2.3	Survey all program teams for use of data.		
3. Facility reorganized with staff re-deployed.	3.1	By June 1, 100% of affected staffing change will be completed. Staff better deployed to support resident care and treatment.	3.1	Check personnel records.	3.	Chosen leading indicators are accurate reflections of good. programs from the perspective of the survey team members.
4. Human rights protection is implemented.	4.1	100% of resident behavior programs and 100% of prescribed psychoactive medications have consent from legal representative by 9/.	4.1	Records reviewed.	4.	Forms and records changes selected will result in "real" rather than "perceived" time savings for targeted personnel.
	4.2	By 9/, 80% of resident-initiated grievances will be recognized/responded to by at least one protection committee member within 48 hours.	4.2	Minutes reviewed.		
	4.3	An ombudsman is available for residents & families by 6/15.	4.3	Appointment announced.		
5. Medical and nursing care records are streamlined to free up more MD and nurse treatment hours.	5.1	By June 15, new medical record forms are in 100% of resident charts and are being completed accurately.	5.1	Sample 25% of records.	5.	Maintenance man-hours and funding available.
	5.2	By September 1, at least 85% of nurses and MDs will increase treatment hours by 20%.	5.2	Nurses and MDs will conduct one week of self survey / work time study.		
6. Physical plant "beautification" and modifications to support new programs are completed.	6.1	1000 square feet of new day program space is created by June 1.	6.1	Tour & measure space.	6.	Budget authorized.
	6.2	New living room furniture and furnishings will be in place in 28 houses by August 1.	6.2	Tour all homes.		
	6.3	All campus lawns are cut to "acceptable" level and maintained on weekly basis, beginning May 1.	6.3	Spot check weekly.		

ACTIVITIES: *How team will produce outcomes*	Responsible	$	J	F	M	A	M	J	J	A	S	O	N	D	Assumptions for activities
1. NEW RESIDENT HABILITATION PROGRAMS		$60 K													- QA System/data can be computerized
1.1 Retain technical experts	Director		x												- Computer staff have experetise to design adequate system
1.2 Develop schedule	Expert		x												
1.3 Retrain staff	Expert			x		x									
1.4 Write new resident programs	Staff				x		x	x							
1.5 Implement & modify new programs as needed	Staff				x		x	x							
2. QUALITY ASSURANCE SYSTEM		$25K													- Union agreement reached
2.1 Assign staff	Supertnt			x											
2.2 Design system	Expert			x	x	x									
2.3 Purchase computers	Bus mgr			x	x	x									
2.4 Create prototype	QA Team					x									
2.5 Collect QA data	QA Team											x			
2.6 Distribute QA data	QA Team											x			
3. REORGANIZATION															- Sufficient volunteers and non-staff committee members can be appointed
3.1 New/changed roles & responsibilities determined	Expert			x											
3.2 Roles matched to job classes	Personnel				x										
3.3 Resources for new roles determined	Supertnt				x										
3.4 Negotiate with unions	Supertnt				x										
3.5 Notify affected staff	Personnel					x									
3.6 Staff practice new roles	Staff						x					x			
4. HUMAN RIGHTS SYSTEM															
4.1 Write policy/procedure	Expert		x												
4.2 Establish new committees	Supertnt			x	x	x									
4.3 Appoint committee members	Supertnt			x	x	x									
4.4 Analyze QA date	Chair											x			
4.5 Review with Superintendent	Chair											x			
5. MEDICAL RECORDS		$3K													
5.1 Identify target records	Expert					x									
5.2 Draft new forms & chart contents	Records			x	x			x							
5.3 Change forms/reprint new forms	Records			x	x			x							
5.4 Retrain staff	Staff Trng							x			x				
5.5 Purge & revise charts	Staff										x				
6. PHYSICAL PLANT MODIFICATIONS		$500 K													
6.1 Design new program space	Staff			x	x										
6.2 Determine furniture requirements	Staff			x	x										
6.3 Purchase materials & furnishings	Bus mgr						x								
6.4 Remodel/construct	Plant mgr					x				x					
6.5 Install new furnishings	Plant mgr					x				x					
6.6 Grounds maintenance scheduled implemented	Plant mgr											x			

$ Total $589K

Develop or Update Strategic Plan
(Lawrence Livermore National Laboratory - LLNL)

This case-study shows how the LLNL Safety and Security Division (SSD) defined their strategic thrusts and turned each into LogFrame plans.

The services provided by this organization became even more important after 9/11. Their responsibilities ranged widely from physical security (guns, gates and badges) to computer security to protection of vital nuclear assets on site. Division leadership recognized the need to upgrade their strategic plans and increase operational effectiveness.

To give you a feel for how an outside process consultant can catalyze an organization's strategic planning efforts, read about what happened when I was invited to guide SSD's RAP sessions. My consulting support consisted of a one-day preparation session with eight top leaders, a two-day training session with 28 senior leaders and supervisors, and a one-day follow-up session with all participants.

On the morning of the preparation session, I met with their key leaders to understand the context of and constraints on the effort. In the afternoon, an 18-person management team brainstormed possible strategic objectives by pulling from related strategic plans. The list of some 40 objectives was clustered into 7 logical categories, which were later re-chunked into 4 categories. These four selected strategies form a useful acronym (CLIM), which stands for:

- **Communicate Effectively**
- **Improve Processes**
- **Lead & Develop People**
- **Manage Strategically**

At a two-day off-site session a week later, I trained a 30-person team. They organized themselves into four project teams that would develop Logical Frameworks for each strategy. They left the session with solid draft plans, and the CLIM acronym helped managers communicate the general strategy with their teams after the workshop. A one-day follow-up was held a month later to review progress and fine-tune their plans.

SSD has since moved forward on all four strategies at a pace that has allowed them to make steady progress but not overwhelm the people who still had their other operational roles and responsibilities.

One of their LogFrames, *Communicate Effectively*, is included here.

Logical Framework for Communicate Effectively

O BJECTIVES	SUCCESS MEASURES	HOW TO VERIFY	ASSUMPTIONS
OAL: Effective departmental communication.	**OAL MEASURES:** 1. UC Contract, DOE, institutional performance measures are met.	1. Finding free this year.	**Assumptions to reach goal & beyond:** 1. Information is credible and has value.
PURPOSE: Disseminate information effectively both externally and internally.	**END OF PROJECT STATUS:** 1. Quality of communications improved, people feel better informed.	1. Customer survey	**Assumptions to achieve purpose:** 1. Employees embrace organizational values
OUTCOMES: 1. Employee and customer information needs are established. 2. Expected methods of communication care identified and used. 3. Forums of communication are established and utilized. 4. Communication GAP Analysis conducted.	**OUTCOME MEASURES:** 1. Conduct baseline survey & evaluate results by March 31. 2. Expected communication methods are developed and implemented by April 30. 3. Forums are developed and documented by communication plan by May 31. 4. A survey to identify strengths and weakness is conducted by June 15.	1. Survey Findings 2. Communication plan 3. Communication plan 4. Completed document	**Assumptions to produce outcomes:** 1. Resources will be available to implement improvements (people, money). 2. Culture supports continuous improvement philosophy. 3. The "Daily Grind" will not override attempts to "make it better". 4. No unanticipated external factors will intervene to stunt improvement.

ACTIVITIES: *How team will produce outcomes*

Action Steps	Respons	Resources	Schedule (in weeks, months, etc)						Assumptions for activities
1. INFORMATION NEEDS									
· Establish team									
· Define structure of focus group									
· ID focus group participation									
· Develop employee/customer survey									
· Review survey and analyze data									
2. COMMUNICATION METHODS									
· Identify current methods of communications									
· Define expected methods									
3. FORUMS ESTABLISHED									
· Consider alternatives									
· Choose appropriate ones									
4. GAP ANALYSIS									
· Identify organizations to benchmark									
· Poll customers & employees									
· Analyze data									
· Develop & Implement solutions									

Reinvent Your Department
(Los Alamos National Laboratory – LANL)

The Facilities Maintenance Unit (FMU) at LANL aimed at nothing less than total transformation because customer demands were increasing and they were falling far behind.

The role of a FMU in any organization is seldom glamorous, but always vital. The FMU at Los Alamos National Laboratory keeps the electrical, mechanical, HVAC and other systems operating so that scientists can carry out their work in support of national security.

This Lab FMU served eight very old facilities dispersed over a thirty square-mile radius. The level of maintenance required exceeded staff capacity. As the backlog of work orders climbed, conflicts increased and morale declined.

The FMU Director recognized that a major transformation was necessary, not just minor improvements. Assisted by outside consultants, his team collaboratively developed a vision, mission, values and code of conduct. All staff participated in the process through a series of brief workshops over a two-month period.

With those elements in place, it was time to shape the master improvement strategy, summarized by the accompanying LogFrame. Outcomes such as "roles clearly defined" and "priorities sharpened" are part of any improvement strategy, and were vital to achieving clarity. Later, sub-teams were formed to create additional LogFrames for key projects.

The FMU LogFrame is interesting because of the specificity of its Purpose level Success Measures. The Outcomes offer a set of ideas about improvement elements that can transform your own organization's future.

Logical Framework for
FMU (Facilities Maintenance Unit) Transformation

OBJECTIVES	MEASURES	HOW TO VERIFY	ASSUMPTIONS
oal Improve facility infrastructure and services at the Lab	1. Conditions improve as measured by standard criteria in documents x y & z.	1. Annual Facility Assessments	**Assumptions to reach goal** 1. Resources available to perform annual assessments. 2. Data maintained/reported.
Purpose Transform FMU (Facilities Maintenance Unit) into a highly responsive, effective, and efficient facility management organization.	1. By 10/31 Annual customer satisfaction rate is consistently >90% 2. Work order response time decreases from current average of ___ days to average of <30 days by ___ 3. Work order backlog of ___ is reduced to <200 and maintained <200 4. Work order age is reduced to <60 days and maintained <60 5. Monthly and annual PM compliance rate reaches and maintained to 100% 6. Employee satisfaction reaches and remains above 90% and 90% of employees give team environment high rating. 7. 95% of all projects are completed on schedule, within approved budget, and with change orders totaling less than 10% of approved budget.	1. Survey results 2. Weekly work order reports 3. Weekly work order reports 4. Weekly work order reports 5. Monthly PM schedule compliance reports. 6. Annual employee survey 7. Monitor project and cost reports	**Assumptions to achieve purpose** 1. No unforeseen calamities. 2. Maintenance staff is committed to program. 3. Good communication among staff.
Outcomes 1. Analysis of strengths and weaknesses of facility management unit completed. 2. Roles and responsibilities within the organization clarified. 3. Key Strategies objectives, and priorities identified. 4. Facility condition assessments for all major facilities completed and updated annually. 5. Objective priority system established for work orders and projects. 6. Plan for improving cooperation and team work among employees developed and implemented. 7. Formal processes established to effectively support improved operations.	**Outcome Measures** 1. Completed analysis performed by 3/1 with customers and employees involved. 2. Meeting with employees where roles & responsibilities are explained, understood, and accepted by 4/1. 3. By 6/1, management team has agreed. 4. All major facilities have completed condition assessment by 6/1. 5. Completed priority system document completed by 7/11. 6. Plan developed and endorsed by employees, employees satisfaction reaches and remains above 90% by 7/15. 7. 100% of team identified formal process needs have been met by 8/1.___	1. Written analysis. 2. Meeting minutes. 3. Sign-off on document. 4. Finished Assessments on file. 5. Document on file. 6. Plan on file. 7. Quarterly Inspections on file.	**Assumptions to produce outcomes** 1. Maintenance staff is capable and willing to do this. 2. Group meetings held monthly.

Strengthen Team Work Across Functions
(ARINC Director Action Group Task Force)

ARINC, an Annapolis systems engineering company, is best known for managing aircraft communications over the Atlantic ocean, and for their airport status display systems. ARINC used the LogFrame with executive task forces. They adopted this tool as an innovative way to help groom director-level staff and ready them to become VPs. Promising executives were selected from across the company, and placed into a Director Action Group (DAG). DAGs were assigned a business initiative sponsored by the President, and given six weeks to deliver. The LogFrame helped them get a rapid start and facilitated discussion across the various functional perspectives represented in each group.

This case study LogFrame aims at establishing an overseas infrastructure to strengthen their business in Europe.

Logical Framework for
Building Infrastructure for Global Growth through Acquisition

OBJECTIVES	SUCCESS MEASURES	VERIFICATION	ASSUMPTIONS
GOAL: ARINC has an infrastructure that facilitates global growth in multiple market segments.	**GOAL MEASURES:** 1. Revenue and EBIT grows by 15-20% within two years in at least two identified international markets. 2. Five Year Plans contain significant revenue and EBIT from international sources. 3. ARINC expands into a new global location within three years.	1. Financial reports that show actual growth over fiscal years. 2. Backlog & bookings figures for future & current business associated with new products & services. 3. ARINC establishes a viable business entity within another region.	*Assumptions to reach goal & beyond:* 1. ARINC will have the capital funding that may be required to support growth.
PURPOSE: Executive Management has sufficient information to implement an effective international business operations infrastructure.	1. Within 6 months of briefing, at least 50% of recommendations have been adopted in at least three of the sub-categories. 2. Within 1 year, 75% of corporate business units have adopted at least 80% of recommendations in each sub-category. 3. Two new product/service offerings identified that are specific to a unique international market.	1. Review corporate business policies. 2. Review policies 3. Review plans	*Assumptions to achieve purpose:* 1. Corporate management is receptive to change in their international operations. 2. In order to meet corporate growth goals, ARINC needs to expand into global markets. 3. Core products and services can be adapted to different market segments.
OUTCOMES: 1. Summary report on company selection criteria for 8 potential acquisition companies completed. 2. Benchmark study of 5 companies (including ARINC) completed. 3. Comparative analysis of 5 companies performed. 4. Alternative structural analyses completed. 5. Presentation completed and Exec Management is briefed.	**OUTCOME MEASURES:** 1. Sponsor concurs with criteria and concurs with 80% of companies identified by 6/11. 2. 75% of required data collected for each company by 7/1. Template is compiled for each selected company by 7/4. 3. 90% of DAG members and sponsor review completed studies by 7/10. 4. A. Responses are categorized and assembled in matrix form. B. Value judgement and expertise applied to comparative data to develop analyses that are relevant or will benefit ARINC. 5. All six sub-categories contain comparative data relevant to ARINC.	1. Successful sponsor meeting 2. Completed templates are reviewed and approved by the DAG group and sponsor. 3. Matrix and comparative analyses are finalized for review with sponsor at July DAG meeting. 4. Feedback from executive staff during presentation. 5. Completed briefing	*Assumptions to produce outcomes:* 1. Outside company respondents are credible. 2. Data are accurate. 3. Eight companies provide a representative and comprehensive platform to conduct review. 4. Responses can be obtained on schedule. 5. Enough similarities exist between companies to conduct a valid comparative analysis.

Develop Information Technology Solutions and Algorithms (U.S. Department of Energy)

Nuclear weapons remain an essential component in the United States' national security strategy. Each year the U.S. Department of Energy (DOE) Secretary must certify to the President that the stockpile is reliable. A team from the DOE developed a new anomaly tracking system to support the Energy Secretary's need to provide this certification.

Since 1992, various international treaties have prevented the occasional live testing of a nuclear weapon from the arsenal to make sure that they all still work. To maintain these weapons as a potent deterrent, reliable nuclear weapons-assessment methods (other than detonation above or below ground) must be used.

Ensuring nuclear stockpile reliability involves lab tests, computer simulations, and analyses of all types. Surveillance of nuclear assets is critical, and the system to do so is complex. Occasionally, an anomaly shows up that needs investigating and resolution.

This LogFrame was developed by a team responsible for developing and managing an anomaly tracking system. Speeding up anomaly disposition allowed for more timely decisions, supporting the overall Goal of certifying stockpile reliability.

Logical Framework for
Reducing Cycle Time for Anomaly Detection

OBJECTIVES	SUCCESS MEASURES	VERIFICATION	ASSUMPTIONS
SUPER OAL: Ensure Stockpile Reliability	Stockpile Fitness Report Reflects More Up to Date information in regards to Anomaly disposition.	Compare current and past reports	
OAL: Reduce Cycle Time from Anomaly Detection Through Closeout.	1. _X_% of ATs Closed w/in Established Limits By. _/_/_. 2. _Y_% of ATs Dispensed w/in Established Limits By. _/_/_.	1. Review Dates from Start to Finish and compare to Metrics Identified in Process.	1. A.T. process performs as designed
PURPOSE: Release and Implement New "Anomaly Tracking" (AT) Process	**Purpose Measures:** 1. ___ Months after Process Release, Lifecycle will be reduced from ___ to ___ days. 2. By _/_/_ lifecycle will be reduced to ___ days.	1. Compare Data w/ Baseline Data from Value Stream Report.	**Assumptions to achieve purpose:** 1. Complex is onboard 2. Management Support Continues
OUTCOMES: 1. New Anomaly Tracking (AT) Process Released 2. PMO Created and Staffed 3. PMO Launched 4. AT Process- Training Program Developed and Taught	**OUTCOME MEASURES:** 1. Reviewed, signed and released to WFS 2.1 Org Chart Released to 2950 Website by _/_/_. Describes roles of Project Manager, Tech Lead and Anomaly Chair; including reporting and Test results. 2.2 Dept Roster includes PMO updated to reflect new employees. 3. PMO begins to facilitate Anomaly tracking meetings & effectively manage the AT process 4.1 Release training to TEDS and add to Course Curriculum for Appropriate Organizations by ___ 4.2 ___% of SEEs Receive Training by _/_/_. 4.3 ___% of System/Component Eng.Trained by _/_/_.	1. WFS # Assigned and Visually Located 2.1 Visually inspect 2950 Website 2.2 Verify additional staff are included in Dept. Roster. 3. Review meeting minutes, track budget costs and scorecards. 4. Visually inspect TEDS curriculum catalog of courses	**Assumptions to achieve outcomes:** 1. Management champions committed to Process 2. Staff available and management approves budget and process approved. 3. Staff want to be trained, management supports training and Corporate Training will help implement training

INPUTS: *How team will produce outcomes*	1. Who Responsible	2. Other Persons Involved	3. Complete by Date	4. Resources Required	5. Information Needed	6. Information Sources	7. Comment
Activities							
1 New Anomaly Tracking Process Released							
1.1 Develop a standard for reporting requirements for dismissing an anomaly							
1.2 Develop and implement anomaly review board w/ defined roles							
1.3 Develop a preliminary investigation process/criteria w/ timelines capability to report and escalate.							
1.4 Define & implement standard requirements for opening documents.							
1.5 Define content & threshold of Project Plan (include risk management & movement of hardware)							
2 PMO Created and Staffed							
2.1 Identify PMO requirements							
2.2 Define roles and responsibilities of key stuff							
2.3 Announce organization							
3 PMO Launched							
4. AT Process- Training Program Developed and Released							

Design and Launch Sales or Marketing Initiatives (Avemar Cancer Treatment in Thailand)

This case study describes how an international consortium planned to expand sales of a cancer-fighting nutrient to provincial areas in Thailand.

Virtually every organization needs to expand sales, increase customers, or open new distribution channels. BioMedicare Inc. is a joint venture company with Hungarian, Korean and Thai partners. The Thai partners are the sole distributor in Thailand. Their focus is on distributing Avemar, a medical nutrient proven effective in fighting cancer. The company also funds substantial clinical research in various medical schools and hospitals around the world.

After establishing strong sales operations in Thailand's capital city, Bangkok, and other large cities, they needed to expand sales into provincial areas. This required a well-trained sales force and a program for educating doctors. This LogFrame shows their plan for rolling out the product to rural provinces.

Logical Framework for
Expanding Sales of Avemar Cancer Treatment in Thailand

OBJECTIVES	SUCCESS MEASURES	VERIFICATION	ASSUMPTIONS
GOAL: To promote quality of life by Avemar to cancer patients nationwide.	**GOAL MEASURES:** 1. Prescribed numbers nationwide increased by 20% in 2007. 2. Product achieves 15 % market share in 3 years	1. Market Report & Analysis 2. Sales Report	***Assumptions to reach goal & beyond:*** 1. No economic crisis. 2. No breakthrough medical method of curing cancer. 3. Quality of product to meet proven medical benefits contribute as promised.
PURPOSE: To achieve greater number of satisfied customers nationwide.	1. Within next year; 100% sales increase in target provincial areas, 5% increase in existing areas. 2. Customer satisfaction increased from 80% to 95% satisfaction.	1. Sales Report 2. Customer Survey	***Assumptions to achieve purpose:*** 1. No serious blame on the product in public. 2. Existing oncologist accounts still believe in and continue to prescribe our product. 3. Customers appreciate new support& service.
OUTCOMES: 1. Promotional materials developed & published 2. Prospects introduced in target provincial areas 3. Sales revenue from existing accounts maintained 4. Sales force strengthened 5. Customer support programs introduced	**OUTCOME MEASURES:** 1. Includes information brochures, materials for both doctors & patients. 2. 500 doctors are newly introduced to product and its benefits through personal contact from reps. 3. 5% sales deviation from existing accounts. 4. By Jan 31, new salespeople hired and trained by experts. Tranining covers product's detail and selling technique. 5. Programs includes medical advice, Toll-free and on-line ordering.	1. Visual Review 2. KPI Report 3. Sales Report 4. Customer Survey 5. Assessment and Test results	***Assumptions to produce outcomes:*** 1. Clinical data are proven and available to publish. 2. Information and data on prospects are available and accurate. 3. Sales Rep. do their job. 4. Adequate number of Sales Rep. 5. Training material and facility are in place.

INPUTS: How team will produce outcomes

Activities	Responsibi	Resources	1	2	3	4	5	6	7	8	9	10	11	12	Assumptions for activities
1 Develop and publish promotional materials															1. Editing is completed by Jan 15, 2007
1 1 Print 2nd edition handbook	Jumpol	Bht 50,000	*												
1 2 Develop new brochure	Nathapol	Bht 20,000	*												2. Well identified prospects
1 3 Create new discount coupon	Nathapol	Bht 5,000	*												
2 Introduce to Prospects in Target Provincial Areas															
2 1 Identify and select prospects in general hospital	Tony		*												3. Sales Rep. understand product
2 2 Meet prospects and introduce product effectiveness	Sales Rep.			*	*	*	*	*	*	*	*	*	*	*	effectiveness well
2 3 Deliver handbook & brochure	Sales Rep.	Bht 100,000	*	*	*	*	*	*	*	*	*	*	*	*	
2 4 Arrange monthly meeting by a seminar with prospects	Dr.Kumpo & Dr. Banjob	Bht 1,000,000	*	*	*	*	*	*	*	*	*	*	*	*	4. Management approves budget by December 31, 2006
3 Maintain Sales Revenue from E isting Accounts															
3 1 Increase time table and frequency of visit	Sales Rep		*	*	*	*	*	*	*	*	*	*	*	*	5. Sales Rep has ability to reach
3 2 Remind product effectiveness and update news or latest improvement	Sales Rep.		*	*	*	*	*	*	*	*	*	*	*	*	prospects or customer in person
4 Strengthen Sales force															6. Dr. Nayada devotes necessary time
4 1 5 new sales rep are recruited to be responsible by target area	Nuna	1,500,000 1st year	*												8. Sales rep. are trainable and willing to sell the product.
4 2 Train Sales staffs on product knowledge, selling technique, etc	Dr. Nayada & Tony				*										7. Dr. Kumpol & Dr. Banjob available at every seminar
5 Customer Support Programs															9. On-line ordering is working &
5 1 Medical supportive calls	Dr. Nayada		*	*	*	*	*	*	*	*	*	*	*	*	
5 2 Install toll free number	Nathapol	Bht 30,000	*												secured
5 3 Install on-line ordering	Nathapol	Bht 10,000			*										
5 4 Rebate discount coupon	Sales Rep	2% of sales						*						*	

Total   x baht

Close Out Projects with a People Focus
(Washington Department of Transportation)

Project closure requires not only wrapping up the documentation at project end, but helping team members transition to new positions. This project plan from the Washington State Department of Transportation (WSDOT) was developed three years ahead of the planned completion of a major bridge construction project.

The Hood Canal Bridge Project Team was established to administer the construction of this major project in Washington State. The employees are in project positions, which means that they will go back to other positions within the organization when work is completed in 2010. Project leadership made a commitment to find positions for both State and Consultant employees that will benefit their careers. They will be closing several work sites, including vacating office space and disposing of equipment and vehicles, at different times as the work at each site wraps up. There is also extensive documentation to complete for both the State and Federally funded work.

"Finish Strong" is a project plan to take care of the people, lining up good positions for 60 employees spread over several sites after this project finishes. Even through scheduled completion is three years away, using a LogFrame strategy helps ensure smooth execution.

Logical Framework for
Hood Canal Bridge Project Closure "Finish Strong"

OBJECTIVES	SUCCESS MEASURES	VERIFICATION	ASSUMPTIONS
GOAL: Effectively care for our Team employees and physical assets through the project closure process.	**GOAL MEASURES:** 1. Employees stay with the project until reassigned per the employee database. 2. No cost for assets that we are finished using	1. Per the employee database 2. Per the finance report	*Assumptions to reach goal & beyond:* 1. Employees accept the closure plan 2. Employees participate in the plan 3. That there is a need for assets elsewhere in State government in a timely manner.
PURPOSE: Successfully close out the project in accordance with state and federal regulations and to the benefit of our employees.	1. Region approval of all documentation. 2. FHWA approval of all documentation. 3. 75% of all employees in career enhancing positions per the Employee Database.	1. Region approval letter received. 2. FHWA approval letter received. 3. Match reassignment results to Employee Database.	*Assumptions to achieve purpose:* 1. Region Staff available to process packages in a timely manner. 2. FHWA reviews the submittals in a timely manner. 3. Employees communicate changing career goals. 4. Acceptable positions available when needed.
OUTCOMES: 1. Complete all documentation required for project closure. 2. Reassign all project staff in a manner that supports project delivery. 3. Decommission Facilities and Equipment. 4. Communicate the plan to employees and region managers through project closure.	**OUTCOME MEASURES:** 1a) All packages complete on time per the project documentation checklist. 1b) All documents properly archieved on time per the documents properly distributed on time per the documentation schedule. 1c) All documents properly distributed on time per the documentation schedule. 2a) Workforce budget meets baseline in accordance with the finance plan timelines. 2b) Changes in employee status occur within 30 days of workforce planning tool date. 3a) No costs incurred for office space 30 dys after it is vacated. 3b) No costs incurred for unused equipment 30 days after it is no longer needed on the project. 4a) Closure plan update newsletter sent out quarterly	1a) Project documentation schedule 1b) Documentation checklist 2a) Finance Report 2b) Employee Database 2c) Workforce planning tool 3a) Finance Report 4a) Newsletter sent on schedule	*Assumptions to produce outcomes* 1a) Project employees remain with the Team until planned transition date. 1b) Any Changes in documentation requirements are communicated to the project office. 2a) Project employees remain with the Team until planned transition. 2b) Employees contribute to database setup. 2c) Employees communicate desired changes to database in a timely manner. 3a) Real Estate Service has staff and funding available to manage property disposal. 3b) Region Stores has staff and funding to work disposal issues. 4a) Project staff available.

INPUTS: How team will produce outcomes

Activities	Responsibilities	Resources	Schedule (in weeks, months, etc)	Assumptions for activities
1 Complete all documentation required for project closure				
1.1 Determine Federal requirement for documentation	Danks			
1.2 Build documentation database	Danks			
1.3 Compile documents required	Danks			
1.4 Complete documents packages for Regions	Danks			
1.5 Compete documents packages for FHWA	Danks			
1.6 Transmit document packages				
2 Reassign all project staff in a manner that supports project delivery				
2.1 Develop questionnaire	Ireland/ Cutler			
2.1.1 Consult HR	Ireland/ Cutler			
2.1.2 Draft questions	Ireland/ Cutler			
2.1.3 Review questions with managers	Ireland/ Cutler			
2.1.4 Finalize questionnaire	Ireland/ Cutler			
2.2 Present questionanaire to all staff	Soderquist			
2.3 Develop Employee database	Melchior			
2.4 Populate employee database based on questionnaire information.	Melchior			
2.5 Consult with Region Managers on future employee opportunities.	Ireland/ Moon			
2.6 Consult with Parametrix on future employee opportunities	Cutler			
2.7 Match opportunities to employee career goals	Melchior			
2.8 Meet with employees to discuss results	Soderquist			
2.9 Develop training plans as required	Manager			
2.10 Monitor database for employee changes	Manager			
3 Decommission Facilities and Equipment				
3.1 Vacate facilities				
3.1.1 Generate summary project schedule for facilities and equipment use	Danks			
3.1.2 Overlay facilities onto summary schedule	Danks			

Hands-On Support and Services

Terry Schmidt and his team can accelerate your success. For more information, including the latest seminar schedules, free articles, and publications, visit our website: *www.ManagementPro.com.*

Free Articles and Newsletter

You'll find plenty of informative articles on our website, including:

- Turn Strategy Into Action -- Four Critical Questions
- Reinventing Strategic Planning
- Tips for Gold Medal Strategic Planning
- The ABCs of Strategic Management
- Scanning the Changing Environment

Our monthly electronic newsletter features practical how-to articles on fresh topics relevant to the world of knowledge work. We also hate spam, and therefore you can depend on our promise to *never* rent, sell, or trade your email address.

Strategic Management Publications

Our growing library of support publications includes the 20-page White Paper *Turning Strategy Into Action.* This features the Los Alamos GIS Team and provides a detailed example of application by mid-level leaders.

The *Strategic Project Management Solutions Handbook* provides an in-depth reference resource of 53 real-life client LogFrames. Includes examples from research and development, information technology, marketing, process improvement, and strategic planning.

Virtual Project Design Coaching

Our team will provide long distance support to you in designing solid projects. You create a first draft LogFrame on our electronic template, submit it, and we will sharpen your project design through email and phone conversations. Create a plan that works!

On-Site Rapid Action Planning Workshop

Convert your most important goals into spectacular results with this hands-on, custom-tailored, onsite workshop. Train your entire team in best practices, build shared commitment to plans, and jump-start your execution.

UCLA Extension Technical Management Program

Join Terry and other thought-leaders at the esteemed UCLA Extension Technical Management Program for one week every March and September. Learn best practices and network with technical and management professionals at the nation's premiere educational program for mid-career professionals. Get latest information at the program's website: *www. uclaextension.edu/tmp*

Executive Briefings and Custom Seminars

Invite our staff to deliver a custom briefing to your executive team and learn to achieve superior results. Go beyond the buzzwords and gain strategic insights geared to your specific issues. These events range from a half-day to two days and are customized to your exact needs. Key topics include:

- Building Stakeholder Consensus
- Integrating Strategic Thinking, Planning and Change
- Starting Strategic Planning Right
- Conducting an Annual Strategy Tune-Up
- Reinventing Your Leadership Team

All of our programs are backed by a full satisfaction, nothing-to-lose performance guarantee.

Strategic Management Support Tools

Our company store offers wall-sized laminated LogFrame grids, electronic templates, wall posters, learning aids, and other support tools.

About the Author

Terry Schmidt is an internationally known management consultant who helps organizations become more strategic, productive and profitable. He has three decades experience as an executive, educator, project coach, and strategist, assisting corporations, governments, and research institutions in 32 countries worldwide.

Terry is the founder and president of ManagementPro.com, a Seattle-based company that helps organizations achieve their objectives better, faster, and with greater certainty. He is affiliated with the Haines Centre for Strategic Management, a global alliance of master consultants in over 20 countries who apply the Systems Thinking Approach® to help organizations deliver outstanding customer value.

A dynamic thought leader and hands-on consultant, Terry has helped hundreds of organizations successfully turn strategy into action. His North American clients include Bay, PATH, Boeing, Sony Electronics, Walt Disney Imagineering, Blizzard Entertainment, Microsoft, Cargill, Transamerica Insurance, the Los Angeles Times, the Caribbean Agriculture Research and Development Institute, AEGON USA, Los Alamos National Laboratory, Lawrence Livermore National Laboratory, and Sandia National Laboratory. He has consulted with virtually every federal agency and Washington State government department. His international clients include Thai Airways, Nokia Mobile Phones, the Bank of Thailand, and Singapore's Ministry of Health.

Terry conducts seminars all over the world. He also teaches adult professionals at the MIT Professional Institute and at UCLA's esteemed Technical Management Program, where he is rated in the top 10% of all program faculty.

The author of seven management books, Terry earned his BS in Aerospace Engineering from the University of Washington and his MBA from Harvard University. His career accomplishments are cited in *Who's Who in International Training and Development* (3rd ed.), *Who's Who in Finance and Industry* (23rd ed.), and *Who's Who in the World* (6th ed.).

He is past president and current board member of the Harvard Business School Club of Puget Sound. He works from offices in Seattle and Bangkok, and brings passion and proven concepts to each engagement.